MEMO

From the desk of Dillon Mills

RE: First-time fatherhood and falling in love

I never realized that being a full-time father could be so demanding, so exhausting—so exhilarating. How can this tiny little girl have so much energy? I can barely keep up. But just when I think I can't manage this active, mischievous two-year-old a moment longer, Jessy will flash me one of her angelic smiles and wrap her tiny arms around my neck and all will be right with the world. For no matter how challenging the role of fatherhood is, I owe my daughter a happy, secure home life. I know it's what her mother would have wanted. And I refuse to let anyone—or anything—keep me from raising Jessy. At least I have someone I can confide in now. My lovely new neighbor, Zoey, believes in me. I just know she does. I can tell by the way she looks at me when I lavish attention on my daughter. Zoey's like a breath of fresh air in my chaotic life—and Jessy adores her, too. Actually, the idea of snuggling close to this warm, wonderful woman doesn't sound half bad....

~FAMILY~

Victoria
PADE

Out on a Limb

First-Time
FATHERS

Silhouette Books

Published by Silhouette Books
America's Publisher of Contemporary Romance

SILHOUETTE BOOKS
300 East 42nd St.,
New York, N.Y. 10017

ISBN 0-373-82188-3

OUT ON A LIMB

Visit us at www.romance.net

Printed in U.S.A.

Dear Reader,

I'm so happy to have *Out on a Limb* reissued. It's one of my favorite books. I particularly like to write about toddlers when there's a toddler in my life. They're usually just so cute and funny that I can't resist putting them in a story.

Jessy, the toddler in *Out on a Limb,* came to life when my nephew, Nic, was that age. There's also a little of my oldest daughter, Cori, in Jessy. Arachnid the Doberman was my brother's dog J.D., and contrary to the stereotype of Dobermans as fierce beasts, J.D. was a sweetheart who actually did let my daughter explore his dental work.

Zoey's large family came out of my thinking about my childhood neighbors who had eleven kids. I always found it interesting how different each of them was, how they viewed life among so many siblings, and how it shaped what they wanted in their own lives. Some thought it was great and wanted huge families of their own, while others felt as if they'd already raised kids and didn't want to do it again once they were out of the house.

As for Dillon, well, I just liked the idea of exploring how a little girl could daunt a capable, grown man left to raise her by himself.

Throw them all together and you have *Out on a Limb*. I hope you enjoy reading it—or rereading it—as much as I enjoyed writing it.

All the best,

Victoria Pade

Please address questions and book requests to:
Silhouette Reader Service
U.S.: 3010 Walden Ave., P.O. Box 1325, Buffalo, NY 14269
Canadian: P.O. Box 609, Fort Erie, Ont. L2A 5X3

To Nicholas, with love.
Apologies for making him a girl,
and thanks for the example of his language skills.

Chapter One

Fifteen minutes ahead of schedule. Plenty of time, Zoey Carmichael thought. She searched through a box of little-used toiletries that was still packed, even though she had moved into her new house three days ago. She found hair-spray and spritzed her wavy cocoa-colored tresses to hold the new shoulder-length, side-parted style away from her face. It was a shock to see herself this way after eight and a half years of doing little more than braiding it or tying it back in a ponytail. Perms were a perk of civilization she had had to do without in Africa.

She turned from the medicine-cabinet mirror to stand in front of the full-length one that she had hung on the back of the door just this morning. A light dusting of shadow accented her green eyes, a little mascara darkened her lashes, and a hint of blush colored her pale skin. She marveled at how quickly a tan could fade. After all, she'd been back only six weeks. Force of habit made her lean close to her reflection and count freckles. She was glad to find no more than the three that had always dotted her thin nose.

She'd forgotten about lip gloss, she realized suddenly. From the vanity drawer she took a tube and applied it to her barely rosy mouth. Then she stepped back to judge the whole picture.

When her sister Jane had persuaded her to buy the teal silk tunic and pencil-thin pants, Zoey had worried the outfit wasn't dressy enough for her youngest sister, Carol's, wedding. But now she felt reassured. It helped that the heels of her black pumps added two inches to her barely five-foot-three height. She hoped she didn't fall off of them. It had been a long time since she'd worn anything but sensible shoes.

New hairdo, new clothes, new house.

New life? she wondered.

No, old life, new goal. "Taking care of me for a change," she told her reflection, as if she might be more apt to accomplish this if she said it out loud.

Zoey resisted the urge to spend some of those fifteen extra minutes unpacking the last of the bathroom things and instead went out into the open airiness of what she considered her loft house.

With the exception of the bathroom, a few closets and a space she intended to use as a darkroom—all running along the north side of the house behind one wall—the place was a single large room with a ceiling that the rental agent had called "cathedral." Zoey considered it sky-high.

The owner was a Connecticut artist, the agent had explained. He had designed the house to give himself the same feeling he'd had in the empty barn he'd used as a studio before coming to Colorado. But now that he had moved on to California and wanted to sell, he'd found there wasn't much of a market for such a house. Because of that the rent was reasonable and there was a pretty sweet option to buy attached to the lease. It was perfect for Zoey's needs.

She'd been able to ship enough furniture from Africa to

make bedroom, living-room and kitchen sections. The ceilings were high enough to accommodate her trampoline, and the lighting was perfect for taking the photographs that would pay the bills. That is, if she ever managed to rejuvenate the career she'd left behind.

She went to the antique bureau beside her bed to get her watch. For some reason, before putting the thin black timepiece on, she turned it over and read the inscription.

All my love, Carl.

She rubbed her thumb over the engraving, as if by touching it she was touching her late husband. The feelings that washed over her were mixed. Love. Sadness. And something else she couldn't quite pinpoint.

Carl had given her the watch as a wedding gift the night before they'd left for Africa. There had been moments, during the seven years that followed, when she had wondered if he'd meant for her to use it to keep him on schedule.

But that wasn't something she wanted to think about today of all days. Right now she wanted to remember only the good parts and so, as she put the watch around her narrow wrist, she concentrated on the afternoon she'd met Carl Carmichael. She had mistaken him for a salesclerk in a camera store. He had played along, right up to the point when she was paying for the lens he had recommended. Then he had introduced himself and apologized for teasing her. But more than feeling embarrassed, Zoey had been charmed. And very flattered that the renowned wildlife photographer wanted her to have coffee with him.

The memory was warm and funny. And Zoey was glad that she could finally enjoy it again in a way she hadn't been able to since his death a year and a half ago.

She turned to the bed where her oversize gray leather purse lay. It was hardly the finishing touch, but she didn't care. She wouldn't be carting it around all day, anyway, and what mattered was that it was big enough to carry her camera, two lenses, and three extra rolls of film. She wasn't shooting the formal pictures, but she'd promised Carol that she would take some candid shots.

All set, she headed for the kitchen. As she was closing the dishwasher after putting in a teacup, she heard the low bark of a dog coming from what sounded like just outside.

"A canine reception committee?" she wondered as she rounded an island counter and went into the living-room area. A huge picture window afforded her a view of most of her small front yard.

Her sign had gone up late yesterday afternoon—a tasteful wood cutout with a banner announcing that Carmichael's Photography Studio was back in business. Just before dark yesterday evening she had transplanted marigolds around it, in spite of the fact that September in Denver was late for doing so. She'd figured the bright bursts of gold-and-ochre buds would attract attention. She was right.

Picking the flowers was a tiny little girl accompanied by a Doberman pinscher who was barking his head off at a bee. As far as Zoey could tell, there wasn't anyone else out there.

She went to the door and opened it just far enough so she could poke her head through and look up and down the street. The block was deserted.

"Hello," she called to the little girl.

The child didn't acknowledge her. But the dog stopped barking and turned toward Zoey. Reflexively she reared back, ready to slam the door closed if she needed to. But rather than charging, the animal caught sight of the bee again. The dog snapped at it and bit off two buds. It took Zoey a fearful second to realize he hadn't taken the girl's hand off, too.

Showing pure aggravation, the child frowned at the dog, said something to him that Zoey couldn't make out, and smacked his pointed nose with her tiny index finger. The Doberman dropped to his belly and plopped his face between his front paws.

So much for the fearsome beast.

Still, when Zoey stepped outside she did so cautiously. The animal's eyes followed her but he didn't budge.

"Hello," she tried again, halfway between her front door and the sign.

This time the little girl looked over her shoulder at Zoey. "Hi," she said, showing no fear on her cherubic face. She had tight blond corkscrew curls and the biggest coal-black eyes Zoey had ever seen.

Casting a wary glance at the dog, Zoey stepped a little closer. Again she looked up and down the street for signs of an adult who might be watching this child. She saw no one. "What's your name?" she asked.

"Jessy," the little girl answered with perfect enunciation just before she turned around to pick more flowers.

"Jessy is a nice name. Mine is Zoey." That brought no response. "How old are you, Jessy?"

"Two," she answered without glancing back at Zoey.

"Are you out here by yourself?"

"No," she said, glancing at the dog, as if any fool could see that she wasn't. She handed Zoey one of the freshly picked blossoms. "Here's little flower for you."

"Thank you. Where's your mom, Jessy?"

"She's gone. I hit her on a hair cuz I'm a fireman," she answered, making no sense at all and snapping another marigold.

"Don't pick any more flowers now," Zoey said firmly but not unkindly. "I think we better get you home."

Jessy turned to her then, and held the bouquet up for her to smell. Zoey obliged, laughing at the officious expression on the girl's round face.

"They smell good, all right. Where do you live, Jessy?"

"There," she said, pointing to Zoey's house.

"No, that's where I live."

"No way," Jessy answered, laughing uproariously, as if she had said something hilarious.

Zoey couldn't help smiling at her. "Were you out for a walk with your mom or your dad?" she asked.

"No way."

"Do you live in that house next door?"

"No way."

"The one on the other side?"

"No way."

It was impossible to tell if there was any truth to her answers, or if the child was just enjoying saying "no way." Zoey glanced at her watch. "I should have been gone five minutes ago," she muttered to herself. Then to Jessy she said, "I can't just go off and leave you out here. How about if we ring some doorbells and see if anyone knows where you belong?"

Jessy stared up at her, with no sign of comprehension in her expression. Zoey offered her hand and the little girl took it happily. Up came the dog to all fours.

"Nice dog?" Zoey questioned hopefully. The stub of a tail shook and she breathed again. "Nice dog," she repeated with slightly more certainty. "What's your dog's name, Jessy?" she asked without taking her eyes off the animal.

The little girl said something that sounded like "knid."

"No help there." Zoey was still afraid to take a step with the dog watching. She slowly held out a hand, saying in the sweetest voice, "Now don't bite that off, killer."

The dog moved closer, sniffed and lunged. Zoey jumped a foot before she realized the animal had taken off like a shot to chase that bee again.

"Are you scared, Zowy?" Jessy asked.

"Nah, not this kid," Zoey breathed in a quivery voice, feeling her heart pound. The dog had gone in the other direction, so she relaxed, realizing a little late what the child had called her. "Zowy?" she repeated with another laugh. Then she got down to business. "Let's try this house over here first."

"No way," the child repeated in as agreeable a tone of voice as if she'd said all right. And that was all it took for her to go along with Zoey as if she had known her all her life.

But fifteen minutes later they were back where they'd started and Zoey didn't know any more than she had before. Among the neighbors that were home, no one recognized Jessy or had any idea where she might live.

"The phantom flower picker," Zoey muttered to herself when they were back in her front yard. "Now what are we going to do?"

"I'm soakin'," Jessy claimed, sounding thoroughly disgusted.

Zoey looked down to find that indeed, the little girl had wet her shorts.

"Take 'em off, Zowy," she went on, pulling her hand out of Zoey's, dropping her stolen bouquet and trying to strip.

"You can't take your clothes off out here, Jessy."

"I wan 'em off," the child insisted tenaciously.

"Okay, okay, just hang on a minute and we'll go inside for that." As she tugged the little girl to her own front door this time, Zoey couldn't help thinking of all the pre-wedding preparations she had been going to take care of this morning. She really needed to leave. "If I get you something dry to wear, will you tell me where you live?"

"No way."

"I didn't think so. But I don't know what else to do with you, so let's start there."

Jessy took one step inside and spied the trampoline. She made a dash for it while Zoey went to her dresser.

"Gimme up, Zowy," Jessy suggested.

"Just a minute."

Laundry had not been a number-one priority this week, and what Zoey found in her drawers was a pitiful selection. The choice was either a pair of red string bikini underpants or leopard-print ones.

"This is how it is, Jessy," she said as she went to the tramp. "Underwear is not something a person buys with

the idea of lending it. Especially not to a two-year-old.''
She lifted the child onto the tramp and, holding her in place,
began to undress her. "But I think the red string bikinis
are more you than the print ones. We'll just knot the sides
like so. And then we'll put this tank top on instead of your
shirt and knot the straps, too, so you don't trip over it.
There. I think we're safe from getting arrested for indecent
exposure.''

"I wanna jup," Jessy warned the moment Zoey was finished.

"Okay. Jup a minute." Zoey dashed into the kitchen for
a plastic bag, then returned just as quickly. She gingerly
deposited Jessy's wet things in the bag while standing at
the side of the tramp to catch the jumping, squealing child
should she bounce too near the edge. Then she checked the
time again. The ceremony was scheduled to begin in five
minutes. Frustrated and at a loss for what to do, Zoey
groaned, "Please tell me where you live, Jessy.''

"I tol' you. There," the child said a second time, pointing out the back window.

Light dawned. "Is that your house right behind mine?
Up on the hill?" she asked for confirmation.

This time Jessy was too engrossed in her fun to respond,
but the house seemed a possibility. It was separated from
Zoey's by only a terraced garden. Even a child as small as
Jessy could manage to step down to Zoey's backyard. And
since her property wasn't fenced, the little girl could easily
have gotten around to the front.

Looking for signs of life up there, Zoey stared at the
modern two-story building. The entire back wall was plate-
glass but since Zoey had moved in she hadn't seen a sign
of anyone living there. She hadn't even seen so much as a
light at night, or a dog in the dog run.

But here was Jessy saying she lived there, and here was
a big dog for the big dog run. If they were just coming
home from a vacation and her parents were busy going in
and out to unload luggage from the car it would have been

easy for little Jessy to wander away unnoticed. It all seemed to make some sense.

She held out her arms for the little girl. "Come on, Jessy. Let's go up there and see if they know you."

"No way." She jumped out of Zoey's reach.

It had been a long time since Zoey had had to deal with a two-year-old. But she'd had enough experience to have the methods ingrained. Very firmly she said, "Yes, Jessy. You can come back another time and jump all you want."

The little girl narrowed her eyes at Zoey and kept on jumping. Zoey didn't repeat herself. She merely stared at her and let her expression tell the child she meant business. After the third jump, Jessy stopped and reluctantly came to her.

"Good girl," Zoey praised as she put Jessy down. Holding the child's hand, she took the plastic bag with the wet clothes and led the way out the back door.

It was a steep climb up the terrace, but Jessy's "I do it myself" told Zoey her help was not wanted. So she followed Jessy as the child made her way through four tiers of purple and white alyssum, ready to catch her if she stumbled.

From out of nowhere the Doberman reappeared, bounding up alongside them. Paying Zoey no attention whatsoever, the animal charged through an open gate at the side of the house. She assumed he recognized the angry voices coming from the front yard. Once she and Jessy were out of the garden she took the little girl's hand and stepped through that gate.

"Arachnid! Where the hell is Jessy?" Zoey heard a deep male voice bellow.

Arachnid?

Zoey and Jessy rounded the corner of the house. A very young woman with spiky black hair pointed to the little girl and in a waspish tone of voice said, "There she is."

The young woman was facing a tall man with slightly

long light-colored hair. Two policemen were with them, one of whom was writing on a clipboard.

"Thank God," the tall man breathed, rushing to scoop Jessy into his arms. "Are you all right?"

"I bin juppin', Dad," she informed him before trying to wiggle out of his embrace.

Holding tight, the man looked over Jessy's head to Zoey. It was easy to see he was the little girl's father, even though his eyes were a pale gray-blue rather than black. They had the same fairly short nose and perfectly shaped mouth. But what was cherubic on the child was somehow chiseled into a striking, masculine handsomeness on the man.

It took Zoey a moment to realize all eyes were on her. "I just moved into the house down the hill," she began, explaining what had happened in the past hour.

Seeming more relaxed by the time she finished, the man smiled at her and Zoey's gaze stuck in the two vertical creases that had appeared in his cheeks. He rested his square chin on top of Jessy's head and said, "I'm Dillon Mills, Jessy's father."

"I thought so," Zoey answered, taking in the loving protective way he held the little girl against his broad chest. He was dressed in tan corduroy slacks and a white T-shirt, the sleeves pushed to his elbows and the crossover-band collar accentuating the thickness of his neck. An athletic intellectual, she thought before realizing it seemed like a contradiction. Then she wondered what had made her think such a thing in the first place.

The police stepped up and Zoey realized she'd forgotten all about them and the young woman who had been arguing with Dillon Mills. It unsettled her to know how completely she'd lost her bearings for a moment, and the feeling was compounded by the oddest sense that the other people were intruding on something private between her and this man.

"Are you satisfied that there's been no wrongdoing?" one of the officers asked Dillon Mills.

Having regained her senses, Zoey noticed that he missed a beat before taking his gaze off her to answer.

"Negligence maybe, but no, I don't think there's been anything wrong purposely done here."

"Does that mean I can go now?" the spiky-haired woman asked irately.

"By my guest," Dillon Mills answered in about the same tone of voice.

The woman stormed off under the scrutiny of both police officers. When they had taken down Zoey's name and address they left, too.

Dillon Mills watched them go. And Zoey watched Dillon Mills. She didn't know why, exactly, but her gaze seemed glued to his singularly perfect profile. His jawline was sharp and his hair was a thick mass of untamed, champagne-colored waves that barely touched his collar.

After the policemen had driven away, he turned back to her. Zoey had to swallow before she could get words out of her throat. "Well, I'm late for a wedding, so…"

"Are you bringing that as a gift?" he asked with a tinge of amusement in his voice. He pointed his square chin at the plastic bag she still held.

"Oh. No." It was ridiculous how slowly her brain was responding. She held the bag out to him. As he took it his hand brushed hers, and goose bumps erupted all the way to her shoulder. Too quickly she said, "Jessy wet her… well, everything, and was about to do a striptease in the street. So we improvised."

"See?" the little girl offered all of a sudden, pulling the tank top up to reveal the string bikini underpants.

Zoey wanted to sink into the ground.

"Very nice," he said, drawing out every syllable.

"Yes, well. I…uh…wasn't exactly prepared." What a way to meet a new neighbor. Worse, what a way to meet a man who was probably a new neighbor's husband. "Anyway, I really am late."

His deep voice stopped her retreat. "I hope the wedding you're late for isn't your own."

He sounded as if he were teasing and asking a question at the same time. His manner had such an appealing charm that she couldn't make herself move away. "No, it's my sister's wedding."

"Ah, I see," he said, nodding. He seemed to be waiting for her to finish.

"I'm a widow," she blurted out, then wondered why. "Well. I have to get going. I'm late already. I said that, didn't I? 'Bye, Jessy." What on earth was wrong with her? Meeting someone had never flustered her like this before, not even when she had met Carl and realized he was a famous photographer whose work she admired.

"Zoey Carmichael—isn't that what you said your name was?" Dillon Mills's voice stopped her on her second step.

She glanced at him again and found him smiling as if he recognized that she was somehow off balance. "Yes."

"Can I replace the flowers Jessy picked, Zoey Carmichael?"

"It was no big deal. Most of them are still there and two weeks from now it'll be too cold for them to live, anyway."

"I could reimburse you, then."

"Really, it was no big deal."

"If you're sure."

"Positive."

"Okay, then. But I promise I will get your...clothes back to you." He broke into a very endearing grin.

"I have to go now," she said almost desperately.

"Thanks for taking such good care of Jessy and going to the trouble of bringing her home," he called after her as she headed back the way she'd come.

"It was nothing," she replied, waving her hand but not looking back.

"And I'm sorry we held you up, but it was good to meet you."

His voice was distant, but it still managed to send a

tremor over her skin. "That's all right. Really," she assured, determined not to be held in the throes of his strange effect on her for one more second.

She could feel his gaze following her, and was immensely relieved when she rounded the corner of his house. What an inauspicious way to meet a new neighbor, she thought, deciding that was the cause of her unusual reaction to him.

When she had stepped inside her back door and was closing the screen, her gaze wandered up the hill again. Standing in the open gateway was Dillon Mills, still holding Jessy on his hip and watching Zoey. He smiled and waved and those goose bumps kicked up again.

An inauspicious beginning is all, she reminded herself, forcing a smile and waving back before she closed and locked her door.

But she could see through the window that he still stood up there watching.

Zoey grabbed her purse and nearly ran out to her car in the driveway. So what if he was a good-looking, personable man? she asked herself. He was no doubt also someone's husband. And even if he wasn't, he meant nothing whatsoever to her. Her goals were a world away from anything to do with men or relationships.

And yet as she drove to her parents' house she couldn't help wondering if there really was a wife. Because if there was, where had she been all that time her husband was outside giving Zoey goose bumps?

Zoey's childhood home sat on a corner lot in a quiet, conservative Denver suburb. Both the street in front of the modest white ranch-style house and the one alongside it were lined with cars. The nearest vacant spot was in front of the grade school two blocks to the north. Walking back the way she had through seven years of school brought a wave of nostalgia. Sleep-overs in that red brick trilevel with her best friend, Connie, catching frogs in the creek, sled-

ding down the hill in the winter, sloshing through the rain-
water that collected at the bottom in the spring, dodging
Greg Pierce's white stucco two-story to avoid all those
taunts about her family.

*You probably sleep on top of each other over there. How
else can eleven kids get in that house?* she could still hear
him say, as he dogged her home.

*The basement's like a dormitory and everybody has a
bed of their own,* Zoey remembered calling back. But she'd
been embarrassed to death, anyway.

Whatever happened to mean Greg Pierce?

He's probably a gangster, she decided as she finally
reached the front yard, which was freshly mowed and
trimmed for the occasion.

Still, she had to admit as she climbed the three steps to
the door, it had been pretty cramped in the house. And with
only two bathrooms for the lot of them things hadn't always
gone smoothly. Eleven kids, and Zoey the oldest. How
many times had she been about to bust, from giving up her
turn in the john to one of the younger kids? Thank goodness for a strong bladder.

The wedding had already started. Zoey stashed her purse
in a kitchen cupboard and resisted the urge to make sure
the things she had planned to come early to do had somehow gotten done. Instead she slipped into the back of the
large family room her father had added onto the rear of the
house when she was nine.

The dearly beloved, she could see, were all gathered to
watch Carol, barely twenty, marry her high-school sweetheart. Actually, Zoey thought, it was kind of nice to have
arrived late and get to look at her whole family from a
distance. She'd been back often enough in the eight and a
half years she'd been married to see her brothers and sisters, but still it seemed strange that they were all adults
now.

Her parents, sitting in the first row of folding chairs,
never looked any older to her. But the twins, Donna and

Dar, seemed to have leaped to twenty-nine. Then came Tom at thirty-one and his wife and baby. He hadn't even been married when Zoey had seen him last.

In the second row were twenty-six-year-old Matt—married and already divorced—and John, only a year younger. John had Matt beat—he'd been divorced twice. Zoey remembered them as ushers at her wedding, with bad skin and braces. Now they were handsome men.

Beside John sat Janice, twenty-four. Her wedding was in two months. That seemed only slightly less strange than Carol being old enough to become a bride today.

Twenty-two-year-old Meg began the third row. Little Meggie, who had graduated from college in the spring and was the kindergarten teacher at that same school up the street. And then there was Denise, twenty-one, the single child still living at home while she finished her degree at the branch of the University of Colorado located in downtown Denver.

We're getting old, Janey, she thought, taking in her sister who was thirty-three and her closest friend. Remember when nosy Mrs. Smith said she saw us with Carol and Denise so much she was beginning to think they were our babies? We told her they really were, that Mom and Dad were only pretending they were theirs so no one would think they were illegitimate. We caught it for that one.

Zoey bowed her head to hide the smile the memory brought. When she could contain it she looked up again and glanced to the left of Carol and her groom in search of the photographer. There he was, right where Zoey had told him to be and using the lens she'd recommended. Good thing Jane had convinced everyone that someone other than Zoey should take the pictures, or Carol wouldn't have had a single shot of herself coming down the aisle.

But even had she not encountered Jessy Mills and her father, Zoey was grateful to Jane for getting her off the hook. Of course she'd agreed when Carol had asked her, in spite of instantly worrying how she was going to manage moving into her own place, help with the wedding and take the pictures. But as usual, she had felt that she couldn't say no. It had taken Jane's convincing her that Carol wouldn't care, and then suggesting it tactfully to their youngest sister, to get Zoey out of it.

She realized just then that the groom was kissing the bride, and slipped out of the family room the way she'd come in. From the refrigerator in the kitchen she took a platter of tea sandwiches and a relish tray. Balancing one on each hand she carried them into the dining room. The table was pushed against a wall and set up buffet-style. The champagne was chilling, nuts and mints were set out and the cake was situated as the centerpiece. But there were no napkins, and coffee had yet to be made. She went back into the kitchen.

"I thought I saw you sneak out."

Zoey held up the coffee can she had just opened and glanced back at her sister Jane. "Good thing, too," she said as she began to spoon grounds into the basket.

"Where were you? We held the ceremony off as long as possible. Nobody could figure out where our reliable Zoey might be. We were all worried."

"I was rescuing a two-year-old with wet pants," she said, going on to tell Jane the whole story.

"Figures you'd be out taking care of someone."

Zoey handed her the napkins. "Help me put these out so the names and date show, would you?"

Jane did as she was told.

Zoey glanced at her sister, taking in Jane's two-inch-taller stature and her paler brown hair cut very short. "Pink is a good color on you," she said. Then she closed her eyes. "And you were right about the shadow. I'm going to have to buy some of my own—if and when I get a few jobs to hold the creditors at bay."

"Are you that broke?"

Zoey shrugged. "I wouldn't exactly say broke. Just in need of proceeding with caution."

"You could have stayed with us a while longer."

"But the loft was perfect—not in the middle of the city, but close enough to everything to bring in business, big enough for me to live in and have my studio, and reasonably priced. If I had waited someone else would have taken it and I might have ended up having to rent two separate places, which would have cost me more and left me having to commute. Not to mention the expense of storing my furniture longer. And with an option to buy, I would have been crazy to pass it up." What she didn't add was how it had chafed to live in another woman's house, even if it was Jane's.

"I know, Zoey. You've told me all your reasons half a dozen times. I really didn't take offense that you didn't stay with us longer. And you can keep the eye shadow until you buy some of your own," her sister said. "Are you settling in all right?"

"Pretty much."

Just then Jane's three-year-old son found them and the cake, and attempted to swipe his finger through the frosting. "Go see where Grandma is, Tim," Jane ordered. The child ignored her and tried for a second jab at the frosting. With an exasperated sigh Jane picked him up and took him to the doorway where she handed him to Janice.

"Where's my favorite brother-in-law?" Zoey asked when Jane came back.

"Bob had the chance to play golf on a private course. He'll be here later."

Zoey shook her head. "I heard you tell him a month ago that you wanted him to be sure and make the time to come today, so he could watch Tim while you helped out."

"You know how it is. He's been working so hard I just couldn't make him turn down this offer, to watch Tim."

"Tim is as much Bob's responsibility as he is yours," Zoey reminded.

Jane laughed. "Coming from you that's really funny. You never shared a responsibility in your life."

"That doesn't mean it's the best way and you should follow my example."

"Oh, I don't know. I always thought you had a good marriage."

Zoey shrugged. "I hate to see you wear yourself out being the one to carry the whole load."

"Did it wear you out?"

"Sometimes," she said enigmatically. "I'm just saying that you have the same tendencies I do when it comes to putting other people first and taking responsibility for everything. Marriage is a tailor-made trap for that. Be careful of it."

"You say that like you never want any part of it again."

"Being alone and only having yourself to take care of has its advantages."

"You don't mean that."

Now it was Zoey's turn to laugh. "I don't?"

"Are you saying that you're going to stay alone forever?"

"Maybe not alone. But unmarried. I just don't want all of that responsibility again." She stepped back from the table to survey their handiwork. "Looks good. I think that's everything."

Jane followed her back into the kitchen where Zoey took her camera out of her purse.

"I thought you didn't want to take pictures today?"

"I didn't want to take the *formal* ones because I knew I'd have other things to do. But when I have a few minutes here and there I can take some and make sure everything is covered."

Jane rolled her eyes. "Why don't you just relax and enjoy yourself. Forget making sure everything is covered."

"Just a few, in case the guy they hired misses something," Zoey insisted as she slipped past her sister and headed for the new bride and groom.

A very tall man was congratulating them and from the back his golden champagne-colored hair reminded her of

Dillon Mills. Zoey altered her course and took a snapshot of the man shaking hands with her new brother-in-law. But hair color was the only similarity between him and her neighbor, and Zoey felt a twinge of something that seemed oddly and unreasonably like disappointment.

Very bizarre.

And more bizarre was the fact that now that the image of Dillon was once again vividly in her mind she couldn't seem to shake it.

Dillon Mills, Zoey smiled her charm—and took a snapshot of the grim stranger who'd put her over his cop-in-laws' lap...

Jodi Cook was the only daughter...

...better...at...has...

...it was fifty...saw...

...of Christmas...was and a wedding...after going she smiled I promise...do...

Chapter Two

This had not been one of his better days, Dillon thought as he brought groceries into the house. First he'd had to do a long-distance cleanup on the Orlando project. Then there was the fiasco with the baby-sitter and the police. By the time he'd finished settling Jessy in and unpacking her things, she needed the two-hour nap he'd forgotten all about. It had been nearly five before he'd gotten to the grocery store, and shopping for a full week—he didn't usually bother with it for himself alone—was a time-consuming affair. Especially with an active two-and-a-half-year-old who pulled everything she could reach off the shelves and tried to climb out of the cart every time his back was turned.

So here it was, after eight, and he had yet to feed her dinner.

"Just play in your room for a few minutes, sweetheart, and let me get some of this stuff put away. Then we'll eat, okay?'' He set his daughter in her room with the new truck he'd bought at the store.

"Honk, honk," was Jessy's only answer, more interested in her toy than her father.

The phone rang as Dillon hit the kitchen. He grabbed it and held it to his ear with his shoulder to keep his hands free to empty grocery bags.

"It's about time, Frank. Where the hell have you been?" he said when he realized the caller was his brother.

"Me? Where the hell have you been? Or more importantly, where were you this morning when I returned your call and got a baby-sitter?" his brother said in the measured, unrufflable way he had.

Dillon grimaced. "You called this morning?"

"Bright and early. Where were you?"

"I don't even want to say it."

"Working," Frank guessed with some authority. "Not smart."

"I know." Dillon stacked peanut-butter and jelly jars in the cupboard. "But it was an emergency. One of the track switchers jammed on the test run for the new coaster this morning, and I had to talk them through the repair. I didn't have a choice." His brother's silence on the other end of the phone spoke volumes. "I know, counselor. It broke the agreement we made about me not working the whole time I have Jessy. But it really couldn't be helped."

"And the baby-sitter didn't tell you I called?"

"She didn't exactly leave on the best of terms," he said facetiously. Then he sighed and altered his tone of voice. "I'm sorry for the sarcasm. It isn't you I'm aggravated with. It's myself and that damn baby-sitter."

"Is there something that I, as your lawyer, should know about?" Frank asked in a way that made Dillon imagine his brother's full blond eyebrows arching as he rocked back in his chair.

"No. Just a scatterbrained baby-sitter who lost Jessy and

called the police. A neighbor brought her back before a search started.''

"There will still be a police report."

Dillon hadn't thought about that. The expletive he muttered was not mild.

"Let's hope no one gets wind of it. How big a blabbermouth is the sitter?"

"My secretary recommended her but I'm sure the girl doesn't have any idea what's going on, so even if she talks I can't see how it could get back to the Whites," Dillon answered, filled with irritation at the baby-sitter.

"I hope you're right. What about the woman who brought Jessy back?"

Instantly the irritation was gone, replaced by a much lighter feeling. "Zoey? She just moved into the house down the hill."

"You know her?"

"Not before this morning." But there had been a note of familiarity in his voice, hadn't there? He went on quickly to cover it up. "She seemed very nice and she must have been good with Jessy because my daughter's been asking all day long if *Zowy* could come with us everywhere we went."

"Which tells me that she made a big hit with both of you. What it doesn't let me know is if she can hurt your case for custody."

"I think Zoey is the least of our worries."

"But do you have anything to base it on except that she stirred up your hormones?"

Frank teased in the same level tone of voice he normally spoke in. But Dillon knew him well enough to recognize it. He laughed. "Who said anything about stirring up my hormones?"

"Hey, I think it's great, so long as it doesn't stir up anything else. Which, by the way, is why I called. I managed to get the hearing set for ten days from now.''

"Finally. I may even consider paying your going rate for this one."

"You can't afford me," Frank said dryly.

"I don't know, I didn't do too badly on the Orlando deal. In fact they liked that coaster so well they wanted me to do a miniature replica of it for their kiddieland."

"Well, whatever you do, don't accept. All the time you've been gone this year isn't going to look any better to a judge than it does to the Whites."

"I've already turned it down." Dillon put milk in the refrigerator.

"Good, then maybe you'll have time to marry your new neighbor. Think you could arrange it within the next ten days so we could go into court with a bona fide mommy and daddy?"

"Sorry. Couldn't do it in anything under fifteen."

"Too bad. Well, just keep your chin up. This will all be over soon."

"Did I sound pessimistic to you? Because I'm not. I'm just damn impatient. This has been dragging on forever, and I want my daughter back."

"You want your daughter back? Why didn't you tell me that before?" Frank deadpanned as if this was news to him.

"I was afraid you might not work well under pressure."

"Right. And who would consider phone calls every day for the past year pressure? Not me."

"That's not pressure. It's incentive to get me off your back."

"Is that what it's called? I'll have to remember. In the meantime why don't you occupy yourself working on the lady down the hill?"

"Who said she needed to be worked on?"

"In good shape, is she?"

"Mmm."

"Well, get to it. My niece needs a mother and you could do with something soft and female to occupy your thoughts for a change. It's time, bro."

"Now you're a shrink, too, is that what you're trying to tell me?"

"Takes a little of a lot of things to be a good attorney."

"All I need is the good-attorney part, but thanks, anyway," he teased. "And thanks for moving heaven and earth to get that court date. Maybe that barracuda on your wall isn't an overstatement."

"Overstatement? It should be my logo."

"Seriously, I appreciate what you've done."

"Yeah, well you owe me. You'll have to design all the rides in my first amusement park for free."

"Absolutely. That goes without saying."

Dillon hung up and took the last two bags to the pantry. But his thoughts weren't on the groceries. They weren't even on the custody case for a change. Talking about Zoey Carmichael had put her firmly in his mind. Again. And he realized suddenly how much she had been there since their meeting this morning. Maybe it was just gratitude for her neighborliness.

"Who's fooling who here, Mills?" he asked himself out loud.

No, this was interest, plain and simple. It might have been a long time since he'd felt it, but there was no denying that was what it was. And it took him by surprise.

She wasn't the first woman he'd met in the past two years who had shiny hair and gorgeous eyes the pale color of seafoam. Well, on second thought, maybe she was the first to have eyes like that.

But she wasn't the first to be attractive, petite or well-proportioned. To have skin like cream and a straight little nose and pale lips that turned up at the corners. She wasn't the first to be funny and charming or to seem unaware of any of her attributes. And yet she was the first who had stirred his hormones—as Frank put it—since Linda's death.

Why was that? he wondered as he turned to the kitchen table and began to fold the empty bags. Hard to say, since they hadn't spent more than five minutes together.

Spontaneous combustion?

His reaction to her had been spontaneous, all right. Maybe it was just because she was such a pleasant change from that gum-cracking, spiky-haired baby-sitter.

But the minute he thought it, he knew that wasn't the truth. His reaction didn't have anything to do with the sitter. In fact, both this morning and on the phone with Frank just now, thoughts of Zoey Carmichael had helped defuse his anger toward the younger woman. No, Ms. Carmichael's effect was much more than relief. There was something about her that hit him like a breath of fresh air after an hour in a smoky room. He couldn't find any logic to it. It was just there.

Dillon realized then that he'd stopped halfway through folding the last grocery sack and was staring out the glass wall at the house down the hill. How many times had he caught himself doing this since this morning? he wondered. But not once had he seen her down there. Long wedding.

Just then a light came on, but there was still no sign of her. Only in disappointment did he realize he had been hoping to catch sight of her. "If you're going to leave a light on a timer, Ms. Carmichael, then you should close your curtains so no one can see it come on by itself." But still he kept watching, willing her to appear, after all.

A crash from Jessy's room, followed seconds later by her crescendoing wail, cut his observation short and reminded him that until a few moments before he had been in a hurry to get his daughter's dinner.

Dillon took off at a run for the nursery, which was directly above the kitchen, telling himself he was going to have to get some control over this strange new wandering his mind was doing.

The first thing Zoey did when she got home that evening was kick off her shoes. Those miserable high heels hurt. Then she checked her answering machine for messages, hoping for something that might mean work. There weren't any.

As she changed into a pair of age-softened jeans and a red crewneck T-shirt her thoughts were on the wedding. So different from her own small ceremony with only her parents, Jane and a friend of Carl as witnesses. And yet there wasn't a doubt in Zoey's mind that she had felt the same high expectations that Carol felt today.

I hope you can keep it more in perspective than I did, kiddo.

Finally comfortable, Zoey emptied her purse out onto the bed. She'd shot two rolls of film and only a few pictures on the third. Wanting to finish it so she could develop all three at the same time, she remembered the harvest moon she'd noticed on the way home. Taking photographs of it would also give her a chance to try the long-range lens and the infrared flash Carl had bought for night shooting.

Zoey went to get them out of a cupboard in her studio. Carl had never gotten the chance to use either the lens or the flash. She'd come across them in a box just yesterday and for the first time in a long while, she hadn't felt pain in the idea of using something of his. It had been a long road, but she took this as a sign that she was over her grief. There was something very freeing about that and she wanted to take advantage of both the equipment and the feeling.

She fixed herself a glass of iced tea and took everything back to the bed where she changed the lens and attached the flash. Then she went out onto the back patio, camera in one hand, tea in the other. Her feet were bare and the tile felt wonderfully rough and cool against her soles.

The sky was clear and the moon was shining in cream-colored splendor through the leaves of a huge oak tree that shaded the house on the hill. She would have preferred to take the shot in black-and-white. The play of hard darks and lights would have made a striking picture. But the roll in her camera was color and she reminded herself that until she had some money coming in on a regular basis this artsy stuff had to wait. For now she had to stick to meat-and-potatoes pictures that might produce income. A shot like this in color, blown up and matted, had a chance of getting sold at the gift shop in the mall that had agreed to take some of her photographs on consignment.

She set her tea down on the small glass table that stood between two lawn chairs her parents had donated to her new domain. Then she raised the viewfinder to her eye. But her aim was off just enough that she saw in Dillon Mills's kitchen instead. Brightly lit and with the window wall undraped, the room—and everything and everyone in it—was as visible to her as if she were watching TV.

It was late to be giving such a little girl dinner, she thought as she watched Dillon serve Jessy a bowl of spaghetti he had taken out of a can and heated in the microwave. Jessy must have thought so, too, because she made a scrunched-up face and shook her head. Zoey knew that a firm two-year-old "no way" was being voiced.

She focused and snapped the picture almost without thinking about it.

"Dumb, Zoey. That was really dumb," she chided herself when she realized what she'd done. "No one will ever buy that."

She altered her angle and took in the moon. In a matter of seconds she had snapped five shots from five different angles, but that still left several on the roll. Somehow it seemed natural to go back to the view of the kitchen. Nosy but natural.

Dillon had pulled his chair over to face the high chair, and picked up the bowl and spoon. Cajoling was evident, and Zoey took a second picture. Father feeding daughter—the scene had a modern-day Norman Rockwell flavor to it, she thought, wondering if she could get her neighbor's permission to sell it.

As she went on watching through her viewfinder, Dillon tricked his daughter into opening her mouth. But the bite he managed to slip in was promptly rolled back out on her tongue. When a glob of it dropped to her bibbed front she spat the rest onto the front of her father's white T-shirt. Another snapshot.

"You really are full of the devil, aren't you, Jessy?" Zoey laughed.

Dillon cleaned the spaghetti off the little girl and made several more attempts to get her to eat. "I'd say she's definitely the more stubborn of the two of you," Zoey said as she took another picture, then reached for her iced tea.

When she looked back Dillon was headed away from the refrigerator with a carton of ice cream and a clean bowl and spoon.

Zoey laughed again. "Nice, Dad, but not too nutritious." Dillon left the perimeters of the shot, and she took a picture of Jessy feeding herself ice cream while squishing a fistful of spaghetti between her fingers.

But where did Dad go? Zoey took the camera down for a second to find him. There he was, back at the freezer, replacing the carton. She lifted the camera back up to her eye and found that again her aim was slightly off. It was his rear end that she had in her sights.

"Cool it, Carmichael. You didn't get the Best Buns Calendar account, remember?" she said to herself.

Ah, but it was a very nice derriere. If she were doing the calendar this one definitely would have qualified to be in it. In fact, it could have been prominently featured.

She raised her lens up the widening vee of his back to where that sparkling hair tipped his collar. And he had shoulders. Big, broad, straight shoulders that would have been a shame to omit for the calendar.

He turned just then and it was his face her viewfinder captured. Zoey's breath caught a little. Great face. Chiseled and handsome and just ruggedly masculine enough not to be overly refined-looking. Very nice.

As if the lens were connected to him, it followed as he sat in the chair in front of Jessy and accepted a bite of her ice cream. Zoey had dealt with enough recalcitrant younger brothers and sisters to admire his relaxed attitude with the temperamental child. Then he leaned back and crossed his arms over his chest.

Jessy took an enormous spoonful of ice cream and missed her mouth, smearing most of it on her cheek. Apparently enjoying the sight but not wanting her to see his amusement, he turned his head to the window and laughed. Almost on instinct Zoey photographed it, feeling as if she were a part of the fun up on the hill.

Then she lowered the camera all of a sudden and closed her eyes. What was she doing? Worse yet, what was she feeling? Warm, flushed, excited... This was crazy. And out of place.

And where was Jessy's mom, anyway? Didn't she do anything with her own daughter?

Film left or not, Zoey told herself she had to stop this and go inside. But the night air was so cool and her house was stuffy from being closed up most of the day. The last thing she wanted to do was go in there and stare at the boxes that needed to be emptied. "So sit here and drink your tea and don't so much as look up the hill," she ordered herself sternly.

She sat down. She took a drink of her tea. She looked at her next-door neighbor's multicolored wind sock. Then a light went on in the house on the hill and drew her attention back.

The kitchen was still lit, but no one was there. Now the light was on in the room directly above it. The nursery.

Didn't they have any drapes up there? Didn't they know that at night they were putting on a spectacle for everyone to see? Didn't they care?

Somehow the camera was suddenly back in front of Zoey's eye. With Jessy slung on his hip, Dillon took what looked to be pajamas out of a dresser drawer. Then he sat the child on a changing table and began to take her clothes off. Big hands pulled her shirt up over her head while he

blew raspberries on her stomach. It made Jessy laugh and
Zoey smile. Another picture.

Down went the little girl's shorts and training pants, and
while he reached for a diaper, Jessy rolled away to escape.
Her father patted her bare bottom and then gently turned
her onto her back again, distracting her with funny faces
while he diapered her. With all of the babies that had been
in her own home, Zoey thought, not once had she seen her
father change a diaper.

Patiently Dillon waited while Jessy tried to put her pajamas on him, half covering his head with her yellow top.
Then, when Jessy conceded that it couldn't be done, he ran
his hands through his hair and slipped the pajamas on his
daughter. She came up through the neck with a giant yawn.
Zoey took the picture, catching Dillon smiling down at the
little girl.

There was something magnetic about that smile, something that made Zoey wish she were the recipient. How it
tugged on her heart. She really shouldn't be doing this, she
thought again, for her own sake if not for theirs. But en-
thralled, she couldn't take her eyes off the scene, which
was touching and tender and funny all at once.

Finally Dillon lifted his daughter into a crib Zoey thought
Jessy was too old for. He bent over the side to kiss her
good night, and Zoey took the last picture on her roll of
film just before he left the room in only the faint glow of
a night-light.

"Good. Now I can go back to being an honorable person," she said as she rewound the film. Then she put her
camera down and picked up her tea.

But the light in the nursery was out for only about two
more seconds before she saw with her naked eye that Jessy
had stood and apparently done something to bring her father back into the room.

This time every stuffed animal in sight went to bed with
the little girl. Then Dillon repeated his good-night kiss and
left once more.

Five minutes later, up went Jessy and back came Dillon again. This time with water.

The third round must have brought him back to check her diaper, but apparently without finding the need to change it. By the fourth Zoey could tell he was chiding her.

He didn't come back a fifth.

"It's about time you caught on, Dad," she said with another laugh.

Not that she was criticizing. She knew without a doubt that Carl wouldn't have done any of what she had just watched Dillon Mills do. No, Carl would have been like Zoey's own father. Busy with his work, absorbed in making a living. Kids, had Carl wanted any, would have been Zoey's job. Just as they had been her mother's.

What had Dillon Mills's wife done differently?

"The woman is nowhere around, that's what," she answered herself wryly. Because if she was, Zoey would bet her bottom dollar Dillon Mills would not have been feeding his daughter and putting her down for the night. Then again, if her mother had been around, Jessy probably wouldn't have had a late dinner of canned spaghetti, and ended up eating only ice cream.

Zoey watched Dillon go back into the kitchen, disappear through a doorway, then reappear. Without the magnification of her camera she couldn't tell what he was doing until he pulled his shirt off. That was when her conscience got the better of her. She closed her eyes. Tight. That erased the actual image of him, if not the imagined one. She counted to a hundred, deciding that would give him enough time to be dressed again, before she opened her eyes. When she did she found him in a white sport shirt, sliding the back glass door open and coming outside, carrying something that looked like a paper bag in one hand.

He changes his shirt to take out the trash? she thought.

Then she realized he was heading down the stone path that led to the terraced garden and her own yard.

Zoey held her breath. Had he seen her out here spying?

There was only one light on in her house and what spilled through the back screen didn't reach the lawn chair where she was sitting. But even if he didn't know already, would he figure it out when he found her? He might if he saw the camera. She stashed it carefully behind her between the cushions of the lawn chair, and sat back.

Where *was* that wife of his, anyway?

When Dillon stepped onto her patio a few moments later Zoey took a deep breath and hoped her voice would sound casual. "Hi, neighbor." She could tell he only caught sight of her then. Thank goodness.

"I didn't see you lurking there in the shadows," he answered, changing course to come and sit on the lawn chair facing hers across the table.

"Was I lurking?" she asked innocently, feeling guilty.

He laughed. "I don't know. Were you?"

Zoey lifted her glass. "Just out here enjoying the cooler air and an iced tea."

"Now that sounds good."

"Would you like a glass?" She knew she was overcompensating.

"I'd love one. But here, I have something for you first."

The moon had risen above the treetop just far enough to cast a milky light over her patio and bathe Dillon Mills's fine features. She could see he was barely suppressing amusement as he slid the paper bag across to her.

"What's this?"

"A present."

"A present," she repeated as she opened the sack. Her tank top was inside, neatly folded, with her bikini underpants on top. She'd forgotten all about them.

"They're freshly washed," he offered, laughter not far beneath his tone.

So he was anticipating her embarrassment. Zoey took perverse pleasure in showing none. "Thanks. But your wife could have returned these. I'd like to meet her."

She saw his expression change to something she couldn't read. He still smiled, but it wasn't a broad grin anymore.

"No, she couldn't have," he said after a moment. "She died two years ago in a car accident."

"Oh. I'm sorry." That explained why Dillon was such an actively participating father. Zoey had the oddest sensation of having lost her safety net. And then something else occurred to her. "Then who's with... Where's Jessy tonight?" she asked, glancing up at his house for a moment and hoping she hadn't given herself away. Her attention went back to Dillon when he took something out of his shirt pocket and nodded in the direction of his house.

"She's sound asleep. I have an intercom in her room. This is the receiver."

"Then she's in the house alone? Is that safe?"

"I can hear every rustling she makes."

He seemed so relaxed. Zoey wished she felt that way. Intercom or not, her mother would have killed her if she had left one of her younger brothers or sisters like that. But she couldn't very well say anything more than, "Well, if you're sure...."

Taking the bag and her own glass along for a refill, she stood and went toward the house. Dillon followed, reaching around her to open the screen door before she could. It put them in very close proximity and Zoey got a whiff of clean-smelling after-shave that went right to her head.

"You'll have to excuse the boxes," she said in a hurry. "I haven't completely settled in yet." She nearly ran for the kitchen. Without looking to see where he was or what he was doing, she slipped the paper bag into an empty cupboard.

"So, you're a photographer," he said out of the blue.

She hadn't unpacked enough of her equipment to make that obvious. Had he seen her out there taking pictures after all? she wondered in a sudden panic.

But before she had the time to say anything, he explained. "I drove around to see how much damage Jessy had done to your flowers and saw the sign out front,'' he said, leaning against the island counter and facing her. ''Why were you out of business?''

She assumed he was referring to the *Back in Business* part of her sign. ''I was in Africa until a few weeks ago.''

''Africa?'' He drew the syllables out in a tone that sounded curious and impressed at once.

''My husband was Carl Carmichael—''

''The wildlife photographer,'' he finished for her.

''You know his work?''

''I have a book of his pictures of Australia on my coffee table,'' he said as Zoey took a glass out of a box and unwrapped the tissue paper that covered it. ''Carl Carmichael is dead?'' he asked then, seeming to have just remembered she had told him she was a widow.

His question surprised her, too. He knew about Carl and not about his death? It had made all the papers and celebrity magazines. ''He was killed twenty months ago,'' she answered. ''He was riding in a Jeep, taking shots of a rhinoceros when it turned suddenly and charged.''

''Now I'm sorry. Were you with him?''

''No. It was one of those strange twists of fate. I was supposed to go—I usually did—but at the last minute he decided he wanted me to stay home and make a call to check on some darkroom supplies that hadn't been delivered. He and his driver were supposed to come back by noon. When they didn't, two friends and I went looking for him. The driver lived, but lost an arm. Carl was killed instantly.'' And why was she talking so easily about something she had yet to discuss this way even with Jane?

''Sugar or lemon?'' she asked, as much for the information as to change the subject.

''Straight, thanks.''

Zoey replaced the pitcher in the fridge and took a tray of ice out of the freezer. ''So, what happened this morning?'' she asked to make sure they didn't go back to talking about Carl.

"With Jess? I had an emergency at work and had to leave her with a baby-sitter my secretary recommended and swore was responsible. With a name like Starlight I should have known better. Anyway, Starlight claimed that Jessy must have unlocked the door and gone out of the house on her own. She said that she searched everywhere and since she couldn't get a hold of me—that part was true because I had the phone line tied up—she called the police and reported Jessy missing."

"You didn't believe the rest?" she asked as she dropped cubes in both glasses.

"I don't believe Jessy can unlock a door by herself. I think the girl just wasn't paying enough attention and wanted to cover it up."

"Was that what you were arguing with her about when I got there?"

He accepted the tea she offered. "I was pretty mad," he admitted. "So if your husband's accident was twenty months ago, why were you in Africa until recently?"

Obviously he didn't want to talk about the morning's adventure anymore. "I had to compile seven years of his work for the publisher, and then there was the house to sell and arrangements to move back here. And I wasn't moving too swiftly at the time."

"I can understand that."

"Would you feel more comfortable sitting out on the patio in case your reception from Jessy's intercom isn't as good in here?" she asked, uneasy with the idea of the child being alone.

"The whole system is state-of-the-art. I could hear her three blocks from here."

Since she didn't have the distraction of serving tea, courtesy demanded that she look at him when he spoke. His blue eyes were on her face and he was smiling almost in the way he had earlier at Jessy. Zoey had coveted that smile, and now it warmed her to the quick.

Then he turned and glanced around her house. "Interesting place," he said, seeming to suppress a laugh when he caught sight of the trampoline. "You're going to live here and use it as a studio, too, are you?"

"That's the plan."

He headed for the tramp and Zoey's gaze rode from broad shoulders down his back to a narrow waist and then lower, catching on the rise and fall of the back pockets of his jeans. More than being prominently featured, he could have been the cover picture of the Best Buns Calendar, she thought.

Then she realized he was saying something.

"I can't say I've ever seen a trampoline in a house before. Do you use this in your pictures?" he asked as he stopped beside it.

"No..." Her voice came out as a little squeak. She cleared her throat and went on. "It's the only exercise I like. I promised myself one for outside, but the ceiling here is so high I didn't see any reason not to put it inside and use it year round. I know it must seem a little nutty, but—"

"I think it's great," he interrupted.

"You do?" Zoey came up beside him—but not closely. His effect on her was too potent.

He glanced at her and smiled again, his cheeks creasing. "I'm a sucker for the unconventional," he explained. "I guess that's why I do what I do."

"What's that?"

"My degree is in mechanical engineering. I use it to design amusement-park rides."

Now it was Zoey's turn to smile. "I'd say that's unconventional, all right."

He reached a hand to the mat as if testing it. Her gaze went along. He had big, capable hands and she realized her subconscious had noted it this morning, because suddenly the image came to mind of him holding Jessy and pressing her to his chest protectively. His fingers were long but not too thin, and while they looked powerful she remembered the tenderness with which he had treated his daughter.

Again she realized belatedly that he was saying something, only this time she was too late to catch it. All she knew was that it was something about the tramp. "You're welcome to jump," she offered, hoping her reply had something even remotely to do with what he'd been saying.

He didn't seem surprised. "Thanks but I think I'll pass this time. It's Jessy who really wants to use it. I wondered all day long why she kept saying she wanted to come down here to jump."

That made Zoey smile. "Jessy doesn't jump. She *jups*. And she's welcome, too."

"We'll both take you up on that."

"Anytime." It had come out a little too inviting. Zoey hoped he hadn't heard it the same way she had. But one look at his handsome face grinning ear-to-ear, and she knew he had.

"That's very neighborly of you," he said, teasing her.

She blurted out the first thing that came to mind to change the subject. "You certainly have a big dog."

For a moment more Dillon just grinned at her. If she hadn't seen him so angry at his baby-sitter this morning she'd have thought he found amusement in everything. And yet as irritating as it was to unwittingly entertain him, she found his easy nature equally charming. Finally he let her off the hook. "Arachnid? He's big, all right."

"Unless something has changed since science class, isn't an arachnid a spider or something?"

"Technically."

"With the exception of being black he doesn't look anything like a spider."

"My wife named him. She thought it sounded like a Greek god or a Shakespearean hero. I didn't have the heart to tell her what it really meant."

He said it affectionately, without disparagement of his late wife's intelligence. Zoey found that very nice. She couldn't help it, she liked this man. "When I asked Jessy what his name was she said 'knid.' I couldn't figure it out from that.''

"She manages to keep him in line, though. I caught her brushing his teeth this afternoon and he was just sitting there letting her."

"Whose toothbrush did she use?"

He half laughed, half grimaced. "Mine."

"So now you're sharing a toothbrush with a dog?" she teased.

"No, I'm a little more particular about who I share a toothbrush with. I bought a new one at the store tonight," he said, again infusing a note of insinuation. Or was she imagining it?

He finished the last of his tea. "Well, I'd better get back."

For some reason Zoey felt her spirits sink. He placed his glass on the counter and she did the same, realizing only then that she had forgotten to drink any of her own.

As she walked with him to the door he said, "I really did appreciate your taking care of Jess this morning. The world's a crazy place these days. Anything could have happened to her, if you hadn't gone to the trouble of finding me."

He opened the screen and stepped through the doorway, then stopped, leaving Zoey standing very near. She could smell the light scent of his after-shave again, and it seemed she could feel the heat of his body. She looked up at the moon rather than at him. "Thanks for returning my... things." So much for not letting him know it had embarrassed her.

"No problem. In fact I'd be happy to do your laundry anytime."

She laughed in spite of herself. "I think I can handle it myself, but thanks for the offer."

"I'm going to take you up on that invitation to bring Jessy to jump on your tramp," he warned in a tone of voice that was suddenly lower and somehow seductive.

"I doubt if she'll let you do anything else." She made light of it.

"Well, good night," he said then.

"Good night." She waited for him to go.

He stayed put.

It was crazy but Zoey had the feeling he was going to kiss her, as if they were just ending a date. And crazier still, she tilted her head up as if she'd accept it if he did.

But he didn't. Instead he cleared his throat and repeated "Good night," finally stepping away and letting the screen close. And yet she couldn't shake the feeling that he had thought about it.

She shut the door and locked it for the night, wondering about her strange response to this new neighbor of hers. He was an undeniably attractive, charming, personable man, but appreciating that didn't mean she was attracted to him, she told herself. It only meant she was human.

Zoey went back to the kitchen and emptied the two glasses. But as she was putting Dillon's glass in the dishwasher she suddenly thought of it having been in his hand, of the rim touching his mouth. And something in her fluttered and set off a sort of warm, tingling sensation....

Boy, was she human.

Chapter Three

Zoey woke up Sunday morning with thoughts of Dillon Mills. By that point it didn't even seem unusual, since she had gone to sleep the same way and dreamed about him in between. The man was like a song she couldn't get out of her head.

She showered in barely warm water in hopes of washing him out of her mind, then pulled on a pair of white shorts and a red T-shirt. But there he was still—something he'd said, some reaction he'd had to something she'd said, the way the moonlight had caressed his face, the way his hair had touched his collar, those jean pockets on his tight rear end…

"Think about something else," she told her reflection in the mirror as she finger-combed her wet hair and left it to air-dry. "Think about work." That had always been a good diversion before.

She realized she'd left her camera outside. Zoey closed her eyes. She couldn't believe it. How in the world could she have forgotten her camera? Her three-*thousand*-dollar, last gift from Carl, camera?

She burst out of the bathroom, ran barefoot around boxes and high-jumped a crate. Her fingers fumbled with the dead bolt on the back door and when she finally managed to release it she yanked the door open so hard the chain lock she'd forgotten about bit a chunk out of the oak edge.

"Damn," she muttered, closing it to unfasten the chain. Again she jerked it open, shooting out onto the patio just in time to see Jessy and Arachnid inspecting the expensive piece of equipment.

"Hi, Zowy," the little girl said, while a dumbfounded Zoey looked from her to the Doberman and thought better of rushing them. Arachnid seemed tame enough, but Zoey couldn't forget that she was still a stranger to the animal. No matter how docile the dog might be, she didn't think it wise to take the chance.

"Hi, Jessy." Zoey took a few cautious steps nearer, nodding at her camera held precariously in two tiny hands. "Did you find that on the chair?"

"Yup."

"Can I have it, please?"

"No way."

Zoey hastily scanned the backyard and up the hill for signs of Dillon. But just as the day before, there was no adult in sight. And no help. She couldn't just grab the camera, for fear it would be dropped, so she smiled and tried to pretend she was relaxed. "Tell you what. How about if we trade. I'll take the camera and then you can come in and jump on the tramp?"

"Yur funny, Zowy," the child said.

"I thought you liked to jump on the tramp." Hoping she looked nonchalant, Zoey stepped closer and held out her hand. "But you have to give me that first, Jessy."

"I'm being nasthy," she informed with a grin.

"Nasty? Well, why don't you not be nasty, and give me the camera?"

The child seemed to think about that for a moment. "Wannit?" she asked.

"Yes, please." Zoey extended her hand farther. Jessy pulled her treasure closer to her pajama top.

"You got hot gum?"

"No, I don't have any hot gum. But I guess if you don't want to, I'll take Arachnid in to jump on the tramp and you'll have to stay out here."

"No way. Dogs don't jup on a tramp, Zowy."

Reverse psychology crushed by logic. She sighed. "Just give me the camera, will you, Jessy?"

The little girl shrugged as if that was all she had wanted to hear from the beginning. "Okay. Save my place," she ordered matter-of-factly as she handed the camera over.

Zoey breathed a sigh of relief, taking quick inventory of her equipment to make sure it was unharmed. Then she straightened and took a slow look around. "Where's your dad, Jessy?"

"He stinks," she informed with a wrinkle of her tiny nose. "I wanna jup now."

But rather than taking her inside, Zoey couldn't help looking at the house on the hill. What's wrong up there? she wondered. A child wandering away once could be excused as an accident. But twice?

"I wanna jup *now*, Zowy!"

"I think maybe that's just what we're going to do," Zoey told her, taking the child's hand. "Come on inside and let's see how long it takes for someone to come looking for you. Nice guy or not, your dad should be more careful with you."

Before she put Jessy up on the tramp Zoey set her camera out of harm's way and opened the drapes on her back windows. Then watching for signs of life up the hill, she stood by while the child jumped.

Fifteen minutes passed before Dillon charged out of his house. His feet and chest were bare, his hair was wet and obviously only finger-combed back from his face. He looked as if he had barely pulled on his jeans before he'd run out. He also looked frantic as he seemed to follow a trail of something down to her house.

Zoey gave him the benefit of the doubt and called out her back door. "She's in here on the tramp."

Relief was evident on his face when he came in. "I think she's taking years off my life," he confided to Zoey after he'd blown a sigh out of puffed cheeks.

"It is dangerous for her to be out wandering around alone," she agreed.

"I owe that baby-sitter an apology. Unlocking the back door is definitely Jessy's newest accomplishment. I made sure everything was locked up tight when I went in to take a shower and here she is—" he held his hand out and opened his fist "—at the end of a trail of raisins."

So that was what he'd been picking up along the way. "I guess you'd better add a lock she can't reach, then," Zoey felt compelled to suggest.

"Looks like I'll have to. It usually takes a scare to make you realize kids can all of a sudden do what they couldn't do before."

Just then Zoey noticed the unfastened waistband button on his low-slung jeans. It put a catch in her throat. Up, eyes, up, she ordered. Slowly her gaze rose to a narrow line of wheat-colored hair that broadened to a smattering across well-defined pectorals. Still, her pulse pounded. Keep going, eyes. This time she found those shoulders that were every bit as broad as they had seemed underneath his shirt, and then his neck, strong and corded.

Zoey cleared her throat and held out a hand. "I can throw the raisins away if you want," she offered.

"Thanks," he said, dropping them into her palm.

She took them to the kitchen trash to buy herself some composure. When she turned back, she found him smoothing one hand down the back of his head, a gesture that swelled his already bulging bicep and gave her a peek at a tuft of hair under his arm. It was all too intimate a view of

a man who had been only partially dressed in her dreams
last night. Composure did not join Zoey's list of accom-
plishments.

"I'm sorry about Jessy showing up here every time she
escapes," he said as she went back to standing at the tramp,
pretending an intent interest in the little girl's jumping abilities.

"It's okay," Zoey just barely managed to say, losing the
battle to keep her eyes from straying to his handsome,
beard-shadowed face.

"How about if we treat you to a day at the zoo for
compensation?" he asked with a straight smile.

"Oh, I don't know…" But she did know. She knew
without a doubt that she should avoid all contact with this
man.

"It's not like you have anything else to do today, is it?"

"I was going to line cupboards," she answered too
quickly.

His smile turned into a grin as he cast a glance at all of
her unpacked boxes. "I was being facetious. I know you
have a lot of other things to do. But it'll all keep. You've
probably been at it since you moved in. Why not take a
day off?"

Why not? She could think of six feet three inches of
reasons. And yet it was tempting.

"I know," he went on. "After Africa the Denver Zoo is
pretty tame stuff. But I'll treat to a ride on the train and a
hot dog for lunch if you'll come."

"It isn't that it's too tame." *It's that I really shouldn't
get involved. Business is the only thing I want in my future
for a while. Maybe forever.* "I just really have so much to
do," she told him, while a little voice in the back of her
head reminded her she didn't have any business and unpacking could wait.

His grin moved into just one corner of his mouth, angling
it up and creasing that cheek. "You make it pretty hard for

a man to make amends, did anyone ever tell you that, Zoey
Carmichael?''

Why did he have to be so charming on top of so good-
looking? Why couldn't he be arrogant and obnoxious and
egocentric? And why did a day at the zoo with him sound
so much better than anything else she could think of?

On the other hand, a day at the zoo hardly meant an
involvement, did it? And it wasn't as if not lining her
shelves was a great sacrifice. In fact, she reasoned, if her
new goal was to please herself, going to the zoo was the
choice she should make.

"Well," she said uncertainly, "I know an out-of-the-
way hardware store that used to stay open on Sundays. If
it still does and I go to the zoo with you, I could show you
where it is so you can get a new lock for your door."

"Perfect," he said in a hurry, as if once he did it irrevo-
cably committed her to the day. "Jessy and I will come
around and pick you up in an hour."

Zoey knew another moment of doubt. But there was no
good way out now. "Okay," she agreed without much
strength.

"Come on, Jess. We have to go get dressed for the zoo,"
he said, reaching for his daughter.

As he turned his bare back to her Zoey was shocked to
see an angry-looking scar running several inches down his
spine. It seemed incongruous with his robustly healthy appearance. He must have hurt himself playing quarterback
in college or maybe lifting weights. But it seemed too in-
delicate to ask. Instead she went to the door and held it
open for him.

"An hour," he reminded, winking at her as he went out
with Jessy in his arms.

And for the second time Zoey was left with the strange
sense that there was more going on between her and Dillon
than what was on the surface.

Henessey's hardware store was still right where Zoey
remembered. It was their first stop. While Dillon was out-

fitted with new locks, she distracted Jessy from playing
with plungers and sifting bulk nails through her small
hands. Then they headed for the zoo in Denver's City Park.

As Dillon locked the car Zoey attached a brightly colored
strap to her camera and slipped it onto her shoulder.

"Thas mine," Jessy said, trying to reclaim her morning's
treasure.

"You don't have a camera, you little turkey," Dillon
said.

"My toorn," she insisted.

"I don't think we're going to take turns with Zoey's
camera." He scooped her up to swing her in his arms until
she giggled in delight and to Zoey's relief forgot about it.
How many times was she going to come close to having
last night's spying exposed? she wondered as they walked
toward the entrance gates.

The zoo had changed considerably since Zoey had last
been there. The most impressive of the additions was the
Northern Shores exhibit, which was where they headed
first. People could watch polar bears and seals both from
above-water where the animals lounged on rocks or through
windows below the surface as they swam and played.

The open air and the relaxed atmosphere did wonders for
Zoey. All of the awkwardness she'd felt and stumbled over
when talking to Dillon seemed to evaporate and she settled
into as comfortable a rapport with him as she had with his
daughter.

From the Northern Shores exhibit they moved on to the
giraffes. When Jessy nearly fell backward trying to look all
the way up to the animals' heads, her father lifted her so
she could sit on his shoulders and straddle his neck. That
was where she stayed from then on, unwittingly entertaining everyone around her with her infectious pleasure and
enthusiasm.

No matter how big the lions, they were "kitties." The
flamingos were "mingos" and for some reason even Dillon

didn't understand, the monkeys were all called Binky. She wanted to take a buffalo home with her and chanted in a singsong until she got to ride the camel and the elephant. Having no qualms, she simply adopted older children to help her along the way.

She was also the biggest ham Zoey had ever met. Every time Zoey lifted her viewfinder to her eye, Jessy posed. "You must have her picture taken a lot," she laughed when this had happened for the fourth time.

"She does seem to like it, doesn't she?"

Halfway through the afternoon Dillon suggested a rest stop. He went for hot dogs, popcorn and snow cones, while Zoey took Jessy to sit on the grass under the shade of huge elm trees. But Jessy didn't stay sitting long. In the center of the grassy area was a stage where a brightly dressed man was playing a guitar and singing children's songs. With the strum of the first lively chord the little girl bounded to her feet and did an imitation of a dance, with her body moving one way, the highly padded diaper in her red playsuit going the other way, and her curls bouncing every which way.

Watching, Zoey had a hard time keeping a straight face. Jessy, she had to admit, had as much independent, funny charm as Dillon had charisma. Even at her most stubborn, she had too much personality to resist.

"You're a great dancer, Jess," Dillon said with a laugh as he came up from behind, carrying a cardboard tray. The praise didn't penetrate the little girl's concentration on the music.

"She really is a character," Zoey told him as he sat down beside her and passed her a hot dog. "I was just thinking what a good job you've done as a single parent. She seems so secure and confident."

He didn't comment on that. Instead he called, "Come and eat, Jess."

Again the little girl didn't acknowledge him. He shrugged, bringing Zoey's attention to shoulders that stretched a blue polo shirt to the limit. "Maybe I should just be quiet so we can enjoy our lunch while she's busy. I'll feed her in a few minutes,'' he said conspiratorially, and sitting Indian-fashion, leaned back against a tree trunk.

He had changed out of the morning's hastily donned jeans into gray tennis shorts, and one bare knee brushed Zoey's bare thigh beneath her own white shorts. She tried not to notice the heat that radiated all the way up that leg to other parts of her body.

He ate some hot dog and then nodded to Zoey's camera, which was resting on her lap. ''Is that what you use for all your pictures?''

She shook her head and swallowed a bite of hot dog. ''Not in the studio. I have a box camera that sits on a tripod there.''

It was his turn to nod while he chewed. The flexing and unflexing of his jaw was a strangely alluring sight. ''How long have you been interested in photography?'' he asked when he had swallowed.

She shrugged. ''As long as I can remember.''

''You mean you were born with a camera attached to your eye?'' he teased with that smile that warmed her from the inside out, whether she wanted to admit it or not.

She glanced at Jessy to quiet his effect on her. ''Not quite. I got one for Christmas when I was ten. An uncle surprised me with it. I felt very flattered that he thought I even knew what to do with one, so I went at it as if I did. Maybe he was psychic or something, because from my first roll of film I had the bug.'' In spite of all the physical reactions she had to Dillon, she found it easy to talk to him. And he seemed genuinely interested in what she was saying.

''I'd like to see some of your work,'' he said.

''Would I take all these pictures of your daughter and then not let you see them?''

''I hope not.''

Finished with his lunch, he brought Jessy over to sit with them. Zoey thought it was nice of him not to let the day revolve around the little girl, as it so easily could have. His wife, she decided, would never have felt neglected.

Zoey watched Dillon handle Jessy's tantrum against ending her dancing to eat. He did it gently but firmly, insisting that the little girl sit in his lap and take a bite of hot dog. There was something very appealing about watching the big, powerful man lovingly caring for his daughter.

But after the third bite Jessy refused to eat anymore. As he had the night before, Dillon relented and let her have her snow cone.

Zoey laughed. "Have you ever heard of something called nutrition?"

Dillon didn't seem to take offense. He laughed right along with her. "Are you telling me I'm overindulgent? This from a woman who has a trampoline in her house?"

"I'm not a growing child. What did you give that poor kid for breakfast? A hot-fudge sundae?"

"I'll have you know I made her hard-boiled eggs."

"Hard-boiled for breakfast?"

"They started out to be soft but I...uh...forgot about them."

"No wonder Jessy's such a skinny little kid," she joked as they threw away their trash.

"Skinny? If you think she's skinny, you walk around this place with her sitting on your neck and see how she feels," he said as he lifted his daughter there, anyway.

"You love it."

"And you take all the fun out of being a martyr."

She shot a glance up at him. His blue eyes were sparkling with laughter. She raised her camera to her eye and caught him in her viewfinder. He grinned for her and it seemed intimate and warmly familiar, a mirror of what Zoey was feeling with their banter.

Just friends, she told herself as she took the snapshot. We'll just be friends.

And then Jessy squealed her delight over the penguins and they were off to the birdhouse.

* * *

It was after seven that evening before they got back. Jessy was sound asleep in her car seat. While Dillon carefully lifted her out Zoey carried the pizza he had insisted they bring home for dinner into his house.

"Aren't you going to wake her up to eat?" Zoey whispered as he headed straight up the stairs with his daughter.

Dillon smiled and shook his head, whispering back, "No, Miss Nutrition, I'm not. She won't eat when she's half asleep. If she wakes up hungry later on, I'll feed her then."

Ice cream or snow cones? Zoey wondered, but her only response to him was a nod that said *I'll bet.*

With pizza still in hand, Zoey watched him go upstairs, then waited for him to come back down. She went into the living room. Its light and airy quality was helped by an entire wall of windows much like those in the rear of the house.

In keeping with the modern architecture, the room was decorated with contemporary-style furniture. A three-piece dove-gray sectional sofa curved along a corner to take up two walls. Zoey wondered how that light fabric had managed to stay looking new with a two-and-a-half-year-old in the house.

A pole lamp arched over from the corner behind, and for a moment she could just see Jessy hanging from it like one of the monkeys they'd watched at the zoo. Not that there was any evidence of it. In fact, with the exception of a crayon on the coffee table and tiny fingerprint smudges on the television screen, there was no sign at all that a child lived in this house.

"I'm sorry," Dillon said as he appeared. "I should have shown you the kitchen. It's right through there."

Zoey could have figured that out after spying on him the night before, but she refrained from saying anything. Instead she went through the doorway leading off the living room into that homey almond-colored kitchen. Arachnid got up and came to her, nudging her leg for attention.

"You're not nearly as ferocious as you look, did you know that, dog?"

"Ferocious? Arachnid?"

"Appearances are deceiving."

"They are if you thought that big sissy was ferocious. He's a lover, not a fighter." Dillon took the pizza out of her hands. "Let's pop this in the oven for a few minutes." Then he turned back to her and motioned toward the glass table. "You can sit down. I'm not much of a cook but I can play host with the best of them. Will you have a glass of wine?"

A little alarm went off in Zoey's mind. The day had been terrific. She'd enjoyed every minute of it the way she hadn't enjoyed anything in a long time. And she had believed it when she'd told herself over and over again that this was nothing but the beginning of a friendship. Still, that belief was going to be hard to maintain if she conceded to sharing wine with him in his house with Jessy asleep, the sun setting outside that wall of windows in a brilliant burst of orange and yellow and pink, and her senses suddenly too full of everything about the man. Why did he have to look so appealingly masculine with his hair wind-mussed like that?

"I was just thinking that I ought to skip the pizza altogether and go on home," she said in a hurry, rather than sitting at the table.

"No way. I'm not letting you out of here now that the kid stuff is over and we can have some adult time."

Adult time? What exactly did that mean?

"Come on. I owe you a little wine and dinner—such as it is—for helping with Jessy. You've bailed me out twice in the past two mornings and I don't think we would have had nearly as good a day at the zoo if you hadn't been there to help me with my daughter, the handful. Besides, it's against the law to line cupboards on a Sunday night."

That killer smile of his was very persuasive. And she was hungry, after all. Couldn't friends share pizza and wine

without it meaning anything else? "Okay," Zoey agreed.
"But only half a glass of wine." Then she caught sight of
the back panel on the stove. "And you have to turn the
oven on in order for it to heat the pizza."

"A minor oversight," he assured her as she worked the
stove and he opened the wine, then poured two glasses. He
led the way to the table, waiting for her to sit before handing her one. "To new neighbors," he toasted, clinking his
against hers.

"And new friends," she put in pointedly as Arachnid
settled under the table, his head on one of her feet.

They each took a sip of wine and then Dillon sat in the
facing chair. "I'm really glad you came today."

"So am I," she admitted honestly.

"And I'm glad you stayed," he said in a tone that suddenly sounded more intimate.

So am I. The thought came on its own and she checked
it before the words could leave her mouth. Instead she
opted for teasing. "You're only glad I stayed because if I
hadn't you would have never realized the oven wasn't on
and been forced to eat cold pizza."

"I wouldn't say that was the *only* reason. But I am pretty
inept in the kitchen," he agreed with an amused expression.

"But you keep a clean house," she offered.

"I can't take credit for that." He went for dishes, silverware and napkins.

Then who could take credit for it? Zoey wondered. A
girlfriend? Somehow that idea rubbed her the wrong way.

After he'd set the table, he brought the pizza over, served
her a slice and then himself before going on. "I have a
woman who cleans for me."

"A nubile young nymphet who takes pity on you?"
Where had that come from? But she knew. From images
of women falling all over themselves to do anything for
him. She took a bite of pizza and tried to pretend she wasn't
embarrassed to have said such a thing.

"You mean like yesterday's baby-sitter?" he asked with

a laugh. "No. Mrs. Culhiddy weighs in at about one-ninety and must be nearly sixty-five. She charges me an arm and a leg and leaves notes if I've spilled coffee on the carpet and forgotten to clean it up."

He finished his first slice of pizza and took a second. It reminded Zoey to eat hers. In the middle of it she remembered the locks. "What happened to the bag from the hardware store?"

"I must have left it in the car."

"When are you going to put them on?" she asked, feeling more at ease with her old-friend practicality.

"Are you worried that I won't?" he challenged.

"Not exactly," she hedged, thinking uneasily about Jessy wandering around outside by herself.

He laughed as if he could see her doubts written on her face. "What kind of a father do you think I am, anyway?"

"With two years of single parenthood under your belt you should be an expert," she said, even though she really would rest easier if the locks were on before she went home.

"Jessy is two and a half," he amended. "And as a matter of fact, I haven't had all that much practice. But I'd bet I still had more than you."

"You'd lose that bet," she said wryly.

He glanced under the table. "Do you have kids you're hiding someplace?"

"None of my own, no," she answered smugly.

"Some of somebody else's?"

"I have a lot of sisters and brothers," she told him finally.

"Not the same."

"I beg your pardon. I was the oldest of eleven. That meant at eight years old I was changing diapers and feeding babies. Instead of having my face and hands washed and my nose wiped, I was doing it for a whole array of siblings."

"Eleven kids?" he repeated in astonishment.

"It was definitely a houseful."

"Incredible."

"And noisy," she agreed.

"I can't imagine eleven of Jessy."

"I think she's one of a kind. Speaking of which...why don't I help you with the locks before I go home?"

He grinned at her. "You don't trust me, do you?"

"You couldn't even turn on the oven," she reminded rather than point out that his daughter had gotten out of the house twice in the past two days.

"I build giant roller coasters that are as safe as a ride in a baby buggy."

"And then can't turn on the oven," she said again, dead-pan.

He took the napkin off his lap and flung it onto his empty plate with mock outrage. "I don't need your help, Carmichael. But now I won't let you out of here until I prove myself." As he went through the living room to the front door he muttered loud enough for her to hear, "I'll show you how handy I can be, lady. One lousy little mistake and I'm condemned."

"Touchy, touchy," she called after him.

Dillon was back a moment later with the bag. "Get your hands off those dishes and come over here, woman," he barked at her playfully, closing the front door after himself. He took a toolbox from a high shelf in a closet at the foot of the stairs that rose from the entranceway. "Watch closely. You may learn something," he told her when she stood nearby.

"Is that so?" she mimicked his tone, enjoying herself and his levity. He measured for the slide latch and marked the holes for the screws.

"Don't smart off to a man with a drill in his hand," he warned as he took up the tool.

"Oh, pardon me. I forgot the cardinal rule. I thought it was don't smart off to a man with a chain saw."

"Him, too."

Zoey sat on the bottom step behind him. She watched the muscles in his arms bulge beneath the short sleeves of his blue polo shirt as he wielded the drill competently. But the most she'd give him when he finally turned it off was, "Not bad. For somebody who thinks ovens turn themselves on."

"*Who* turn themselves on?" he asked as if he had missed hearing a juicy piece of gossip.

"Very funny."

"My talents are many and varied," he assured her.

"I'll make note."

"Please do."

But what she made note of was his firm buns in the tight tennis shorts as he turned them her way to screw half of the new latch onto the door. Moving her view to his sinewy, hairy bare legs wasn't much better, so she kept her glance going downward until she stared at his feet, encased in short white socks and well-worn tennis shoes.

"You're not paying attention," he said over his shoulder.

Zoey snapped to. "I just thought you dropped something," she lied.

"There are no flaws in perfection," he informed loftily.

She silently agreed because perfection was just what he seemed—nice, caring, sensitive, great body, knockout face, funny...

"Hold your applause until the end," he said as if he'd been reading her mind, but with so much self-mockery she was convinced he was unaware of all his attributes.

The drill sounded again as he bored holes for the wall part of the latch. Four screws held the plate in place and he was finished. Pushing the lock into the casing with a flourish he said, "Presto," turned and wiggled his eyebrows at her. "You're my captive now."

"Not with two other escape routes open," she answered, reminding him of the remaining doors.

"Come along, Doubting Thomas Carmichael," he said

as he tucked his toolbox under his arm, picked up the hardware sack in his hand and took her elbow with his free hand.

Zoey could feel the heat of his body through his shirt and it did strange things to her stomach. Or maybe it was the pizza, she thought hopefully.

He escorted her into the kitchen, where he made quick work of the sliding door. Then, again holding her arm, he took her into a connecting room.

It had probably been intended as a housekeeper's suite originally, but Dillon used it as his office. A huge drafting table dominated the space smack dab in the center, with several filing cabinets lining two walls. The third was a gallery of sorts, displaying framed photographs of amusement-park rides.

"Are those yours?" she asked, nodding toward the pictures as he released her arm and went to work.

"Are you trying to change the subject before conceding that I was unfairly accused of not being able to secure this place for a two-and-a-half-year-old?"

Zoey raised her hands, palms out. "I give up, I give up."

He grinned at her over his shoulder. "Say: I was wrong, oh mighty master of the drill, no one can do it like you can."

She laughed but struggled with embarrassment at his innuendo. "I was wrong, Mills. You're better with security than you are with cooking," she paraphrased.

"Not quite what I was hoping to hear, but I suppose it will have to do."

As he drilled she went to the wall of pictures. The photographer had had respect for Dillon's designs, was the first thing she thought, because all of them looked like the mechanical miracles they were rather than mere amusement-park rides.

She could tell roller coasters were his specialty because there were over a dozen of them. There was also a runaway train, some sort of spiral from which cars swung out, two elaborate rocket ships, an alien spacecraft, a quaking mine-shaft ride and several log rides that seemed to drop cars straight down.

"I hope you're standing there speechless with awe," he said just before the click of the toolbox lid sounded.

Zoey glanced over at him, finding that while she'd been intent on his work, Dillon had finished the lock.

He came up beside her, very close beside her. Zoey went back to staring at the pictures, ignoring a little skitter that ran up her spine when he casually draped his arm across her shoulders. "They're beautiful," she said, not knowing herself if what was in her voice was wonderment or something else.

"Thank you." He reached across her to point to an enormous roller coaster. "That's my latest baby. It's in Orlando."

Zoey could do no more than nod. She could smell traces of his after-shave mingling with a scent that was all his own, masculine and sensual and…and it tightened up her insides something fierce. She forced herself to look more closely at the picture and listen to his description of two-hundred-foot, fifty-degree drops and eighty-mile-per-hour speeds.

"I just finished it. Yesterday was its first public run," he said in conclusion.

That accounted for the date in the lower right hand corner of the picture. "So this is the history of your career," she managed.

"This is it," he said with just the right amount of humble pride. "That coaster up in the left corner was my first."

Zoey glanced there. Then she looked at each picture in turn, this time noting the dates and how regular they were. But there was a gap between this last ride in Orlando and the ones before.

"What did you do in between the mine shaft and this last one? Take a long vacation?" she joked.

"Mmm, sort of," he said quietly.

It occurred to Zoey that that span of time had come right after the death of his wife. She wished she could bite off her tongue. Instead she said, "Well, I'm impressed. These are really something."

"Want to be my saleswoman?" he teased, playfully running a knuckle down the side of her face.

Zoey didn't know which was worse, her embarrassment over not putting two and two together about the lapse in his work, or her involuntary reaction to his touch. Either way, she decided, it was time to escape.

"I really have to get home." Where had that raspy voice come from?

"Stay and have another glass of wine," he invited in a low baritone that sounded every bit as intimate as hers had.

"No, I honestly can't." That one had been firm. He couldn't know what an effect it had taken to accomplish it.

"Then let me get the intercom and I'll walk you down the hill."

"That's okay," she said too fast.

"No arguments, Carmichael," he chastised in a way that made it sound like an endearment. He kept his arm around her until they reached the doorway, where he let go of her so she could go through first. Zoey made a beeline for the sliding-glass door in the kitchen, trying to figure out the new lock while he got the intercom receiver from the marble counter.

Just before he reached her the door slid open. She breathed a silent sigh of relief and actually thought of making a run for it down the hill. This man's effect on her was much, much too potent. But of course she didn't. Instead she waited for him to come up beside her on the brick path that led down to the garden.

"Well, let's hope you've seen the last of my daughter's impromptu visits," he said as they descended the steps.

"It isn't that I mind," she answered, keeping her distance. "I just worried that she might go somewhere else instead and get lost."

"Mmm," he agreed as they stepped onto her lawn and crossed the short distance to her patio. "Thanks again for coming with us today."

"I enjoyed it. Thank you for inviting me. And for lunch and dinner." She felt as breathless as if they had just walked a mile instead of several feet. But at least she was there, fumbling with her key at her own back door, with the screen against her shoulder. Only another moment and she would be home free.

She unlocked the door and pushed it open. The single lamp beside her couch had automatically turned on, casting a low light on Dillon's features. She tried not to look. Failing that she tried not to like it so much.

"Well. Good night."

He didn't say anything. Instead he stared down into her face, his expression serene, amused, understanding. He moved closer and stopped, waiting, she knew, to see if she would move away.

She meant to. She told herself to. But somehow it just didn't happen.

So on he came the rest of the way, taking her lips with his. His mouth was warm and just slightly moist. There was no demand in the kiss, just a questioning sort of greeting. A beginning.

And then it was over. Too soon, she thought at the same moment she was telling herself it should never have happened at all.

"Good night, Zoey," he said finally, smiling slightly, his blue eyes scanning her face as if looking for something.

"Good night," she answered, realizing belatedly that she had already said it once.

He dipped in quickly for a second kiss. A bare brushing of his mouth against hers that seemed to tell her not to think the first one was an isolated incident. Then he was gone, across her patio and up the terraced garden to his own yard. And this time it wasn't his derriere that her eyes followed. It was the whole of him, tall, muscular, perfectly proportioned and more. This time it was the man inside of the body that she saw, as well.

She closed her eyes and shook herself. Then she went inside and closed her door against him.

She didn't want these feelings. She didn't want these thoughts. A man alone with a child was a two-fold trap for someone who always thought she had to take care of things. And that was a trap she was not going to fall into. No matter what.

Chapter Four

What was it she'd said to Jane at the wedding? Zoey thought, as she looked at the balance in her checkbook. That she wasn't exactly broke? It needed to be amended. When a person had more bills than money to pay them, she qualified as broke. Three had just come in the mail. Two she might be able to swing, but that third was another story.

Zoey knew a moment's regret at having agreed with Carl that in the event of either of their deaths all of the other's assets would go to a save-the-wildlife fund. But who had ever thought it would cost so much to move back to the States and set up housekeeping and a business? And who had ever thought that all of her old clients would be so happy with the photographers they'd used in the past eight years that not one of them would be interested in breathing new life into her business? Not Zoey.

She took a look at the three bills again. A second notice

from the shipping company she'd used, a third from a credit card company, and one from her medical insurance.

"Let's just hope I don't get sick or have an accident until I get a job," she muttered as she put the insurance bill in a drawer.

The doorbell rang just then, and with a silent plea for it to signal a paying customer, she answered it. Standing outside was a tall, paunchy man in a cheap pin-striped suit. His face was ruddy and jowly, and both his bushy eyebrows and his thick hair were snow-white.

Zoey's first thought was that he looked like a kindly, not too well-off, older gentleman, and she hoped he didn't want portraits of himself that would make him look like Cary Grant. Then again, beggars couldn't be choosers, and if that was what he wanted she'd do a lot of retouching.

"I'm looking for the photographer," he said when she'd greeted him.

A polyester-dressed answer to her prayers. "Won't you come in?"

Wearing jean shorts and a sweatshirt, she had to admit she didn't look too professional. But then most customers called first. She held her hand out to him. "I'm Zoey Carmichael." He took the hand but eyed her up and down dubiously, so she added, "The photographer. I apologize for my appearance, but I'm still in the process of settling in."

He nodded, glancing around at the stacks of boxes still littering the place. "Your sign said you were open for business."

"I am. But since it only went up on Friday I haven't attracted too much work yet. I'm unpacking in the meantime, but I assure you it can wait." She headed into the living-room section. "Please sit down and tell me what I can do for you," she said, taking the overstuffed navy-blue chair so that he could have the matching sofa that stood at a right angle. With the coffee table in front of them both and an end table with a bean-pot lamp between, this part of the house was basically finished.

"My name is Harold Miflin," he said finally. "I'm an investigator."

The shipping company sent investigators when a bill was overdue?

"I've been assigned to the Jessica Mills custody case," he went on when she didn't say anything.

"The Jessica Mills custody case?" she repeated, even more confused.

"She's the little girl from that house up the hill behind you."

"Yes, I know who she is. But I don't know what custody case you're talking about."

"Her father, Dillon Mills, does not have legal custody of the child. Her maternal grandparents do. The situation has been temporary, but the courts have been petitioned to make the arrangement permanent. And as I've said, I've been assigned to investigate."

"What exactly are you investigating?"

"Whether or not the father is fit to have custody."

The words seemed to hang there in the air with a life of their own. Dillon an unfit father? She didn't believe it. But what she said was, "I don't understand."

"The child was taken away from Mr. Mills and placed in the custody of Richard and Evelyn White two years ago," he explained, as if that would clear it up.

"Taken away? Why? What did he do?"

"All I can say is that it was a court decision."

"But Jessy is with her father now. She has been all weekend."

"Which is why we're interested in employing you at this time. Mr. Mills has been granted limited visitation rights. He will have the child for the remainder of this week. My assignment is to keep tabs on them, but I have another case that's reached a crucial stage. When I saw your sign go up on Friday I suggested to my office that what we have here is an opportunity for nearly round-the-clock documentation of what is actually going on up the hill—at least what can be seen through those windows on the back of the house and anything that goes on out in the yard or the neighborhood—without putting any more of a strain on our already overburdened manpower. My supervisor approved the idea and I'm here to offer you the job.''

"The courts want to hire me to take covert pictures of my neighbor?" Zoey paraphrased. She needed a job, but she didn't care for the sound of this one. She liked Dillon as a person and as a father. Taking clandestine snapshots just to finish out her film Saturday night was bad enough. This seemed downright sleazy.

"I'm not asking you to stack the deck against the man,'' Miflin went on. "What we need are pictures of everything that's happening there, good or bad—''

Zoey cut him off when something occurred to her. "Just how bad—what exactly is he accused of?''

"I can't go into the details, Ms. Carmichael. I can only tell you what I have.''

"Is he accused of molesting Jessy?" she demanded.

Miflin didn't answer readily. When he did it was as if he were doing something he shouldn't. "No. There's no molestation involved.''

"Physical abuse? Neglect?''

"I really can't say anymore, except that this is not a criminal case. But if he's a good father and the environment in which he would be raising the child is a better one than what she has with her grandparents, your pictures may very well show it. The Whites have people to testify on their behalf—a live-in housekeeper and maids who have witnessed what goes on between them and the child. It's possible that you could be providing positive evidence on Mr. Mills's behalf to counterbalance it.''

Or not. Zoey couldn't help remembering the pictures she'd already taken. Not to mention what she had seen firsthand.

Everything suddenly took on a new light. Shouldn't he have been more conscientious about what he fed his daughter and when? Shouldn't he have made sure any baby-sitter he left the child with was responsible enough to watch Jessy more carefully? Shouldn't he have considered her claim that the little girl could open the door by herself more seriously and taken precautions, just in case? Shouldn't he have watched her more closely himself? And hadn't it been Zoey who suggested adding childproof locks and then insisted they install them last night? Would any of it have been done if she hadn't?

"Ms. Carmichael?" Miflin said when she hadn't spoken in some time. "I'll need to know if you'll take the job."

"What exactly would it entail?" she heard herself say as if she were listening from a distance.

"Just what I've told you. We'd like photographs of everything you can see from when they get up in the morning to when they go to bed at night. Give us an idea of his lifestyle, of the kind of father he is, of the environment in which Jessica would be living. Are there women going in and out, spending the night? Is Jessica locked in her room for hours on end? Does he strike her? Does he keep her clean and well-clothed? Is she well fed?" He paused. "Of course it's important that Mr. Mills not be tipped off as to what's going on. We can't have staged good behavior. That wouldn't serve the child's best interest."

The child's best interest.

That phrase echoed in Zoey's mind. The job still seemed sleazy. But she liked Jessy. And even if she didn't, even if the little girl were a total stranger, how could she live with herself if anything really harmful was going on up there and she didn't do anything about it?

"I've been authorized to pay whatever you ask," Miflin added.

But it wasn't the money that carried any weight at that moment. It was Jessy.

Zoey took a deep breath and said softly, "All right. I'll do it."

Miflin again glanced around at her unpacked boxes and the general clutter. "And you'll be able to start immediately?"

"Yes," she answered without enthusiasm.

"Do you have any other questions?"

"No." Zoey felt numb. How could this be? Dillon had seemed like such a nice guy. Then again, maybe he was, she reminded herself, and if nothing bad was going on, all her pictures would show that Dillon was a good father. But somehow that seemed hard to believe now. After all, hadn't the court already taken Jessy away from him?

Zoey was late in noticing that Harold Miflin had stood and headed for the front door. "I've taken your phone number from the sign. I'll be in touch."

Zoey let him out, thinking he sounded like someone out of a bad movie. But then that was what this whole thing seemed like.

Then he was gone. And Zoey was employed.

She let out a wry, mirthless laugh. "Guess all that time hiding in bushes taking pictures of unsuspecting animals is going to come in handy."

But given the choice between no money and proving Dillon Mills an unfit father, she'd have picked going without money.

When Jessy went down for her nap that afternoon Dillon headed for his own bedroom, dragging a battered old trunk behind him. He kicked a pair of tennis shoes into his closet and closed the door. Then he moved on to the matching one beside it. Linda's closet.

He hadn't opened that other door once in the entire year since he'd gotten back here. He half expected that when he did the scent of her favorite perfume would slap him in the face. But two years' worth of mustiness was all he smelled.

And while a wave of sadness washed through him, it was a mild thing, powerless.

"Hi, honey," he said as he stepped into the closet. Strange how easy the words came. Stranger still how painlessly.

Linda would have been horrified to see the walk-in space the way it was. She had always kept it in perfect order—shoes all lined up, hangers evenly spaced. But her mother and Frank's wife, Sharon, had come a few months after the accident and gathered up all of Linda's belongings. They had taken what they wanted for themselves and given away mementos and clothes to anyone else they thought might like to have them. The rest had been stuffed in this closet, as he'd told them to do, until a time when Dillon could face disposing of it himself. And today was that time.

He started with the boxes that were cluttering the floor. Hot rollers, curling irons, hairbrushes and combs were in the first one. A lot of stuff for such short hair, he thought, remembering the way she had worn it cut close at her nape so all she had to do was put a little curl in the top. For some reason it brought to mind Zoey's wildly wavy shoulder-length hair. It suited her slightly off-centeredness the same way Linda's had suited her practicality.

The next box was much smaller. It held makeup and perfume. Linda hadn't been one for much of the stuff. As he dragged it out he was tempted to open a bottle of the perfume. Why was that? To invite memories, or to test how far he'd come since Frank had told him Linda hadn't made it. Either way it was an unnecessary exercise, he decided and relegated that box as trash.

Farther back into the closet he came across two boxes of lingerie. That twisted his heart some. The first was full of nightgowns. Some flannel and faded, some she'd worn on special occasions, a few he'd bought as gifts or jokes. Thoughts of the nights they'd shared came then, and he found a spot of sadness in himself that was slightly more raw than the rest. Not much, but a little. Eager to move on,

he sorted through them, putting a few in the makeup box
for disposal and the rest in the trunk for charity.

The other box held underwear. But this time rather than
thoughts of Linda, there came to his mind those bikini pants
of Zoey's that Jessy had come home wearing on Saturday.
He couldn't help smiling. He'd never seen anyone blush
quite as deeply as Zoey had when Jess had lifted up that
shirt to show him. But he liked what that seemed to say
about her—modest in public, sexy in private.

Dillon scratched his chin. What the hell was he doing
thinking things like that?

He reached for the other boxes shoved still farther back
in the closet, trying to ignore the picture his imagination
conjured of what Zoey would look like in those bikini
pants. But then there were a lot of things about Zoey Carmichael that were hard to get out of his mind these days.
He sighed and shook his head, forcing his attention back
to the task at hand.

Linda's sweaters and shoes filled two of the last three
boxes. The clothes were big, bulky things. Linda had been
a fairly large lady, tall and well-built. Zoey could never
match up to that. But somehow it didn't matter. She was
short and compact and there wasn't a thing about her that
he didn't find attractive. "Obviously, or you wouldn't have
been thinking about how she looks in her underwear," he
said wryly to himself.

The sweaters and shoes went into the charity trunk. Then
Dillon turned his attention to the last box, filled with out-
dated women's magazines. Linda kept the ones that had
recipes or exercises or knitting patterns or decorating ideas
she had wanted to try. But rather than picturing Linda as
he looked down at them, he remembered a couple of magazines tossed on top of one of Zoey's moving boxes. All
photography-oriented.

Her career was important to her, he thought, recalling
some of the things she had said. He found something stim-

ulating about that. Something that made her admiration of his own work seem more flattering.

But fast on that came a twinge of guilt. It wasn't that he thought less of Linda for not having a career. He hadn't. Nor had he doubted her intelligence or abilities or capabilities for a minute. Or ever wished she had been anything but what she was.

But the two women were definitely different, he thought as he stood and began to take Linda's clothes off hangers. As different as the magazines they read. Linda had been the earth-mother type. She baked bread, canned fruit, made a nice home. She had wanted Dillon and then Jessy to be her career. And that had been fine with him. In fact it had been damn nice having someone who took care of everything and left him free to concentrate on work or do little more than play with Jessy when he came home.

But as much as he had liked it and loved Linda, when he thought about a woman in his life now the same thing didn't appeal to him. Why was that?

Two incredibly tough years was why.

If he hadn't taken such a passive role around the house and in raising Jessy he might not be in this custody mess. Certainly he wouldn't be at a loss about things like baby-sitters or cooking or grocery shopping or organizing a house and a two-and-a-half-year-old's schedule or any of the other multitude of things Linda had done. And sitting back and being taken care of was not the way he wanted to live anymore. He wanted an active role in his daughter's life, in his own.

But that wasn't all there was to it. He just plain wasn't the same person at thirty-eight that he'd been when he'd fallen in love with Linda in college. Other things in a woman appealed to him now.

Zoey appealed to him now.

He might as well admit it. Why skirt the issue when she'd been riding around in his head almost every minute since he'd set eyes on her? When she was actually the

reason today had suddenly become the day to clean out this
closet?

Somewhere along the way, he realized, his grief had
ended and his heart had healed. Intellectually he'd thought
that was the case, but he hadn't put it to the test by opening
the door to this closet. There wasn't a reason to. His
thoughts for the future had all revolved around Jessy and
his work.

And why not? The women he'd met since the accident
had been nice enough. Sweet enough. Intelligent enough.
Pretty enough. Enjoyable enough. But no one had struck
him as special. No one had lingered in his thoughts. No
one had had just that right mixture of humor and serious-
ness. No one had felt like she fit. Until now.

He was attracted to Zoey. Excited by her. Intrigued by
her. Interested in her. Amused by her. Aroused by her.
Comfortable with her. But not in the same way any of it
had been with Linda. No, Zoey felt like a fresh start.

And he was ready for fresh starts all the way around.

There were a few things in the top of the closet that
Dillon took down and sorted through. Old novels went into
the charity trunk, as did maternity clothes and swimming
suits. A bag full of shoulder pads went into the trash, while
a box of letters he'd written to her over the years and pictures that meant something special to her he put on the bed.
Those he'd save for Jessy when she was older.

And then there was nothing left in the closet but lint and
debris.

Dillon had expected it to hurt like hell to look in there
and see it empty, see the last of Linda gone. But it didn't.
Clothes and shoes and things weren't Linda. The important
things about her were still here—in his heart, in Jessy's
face and movements and expressions.

But the time had come to acknowledge that Linda really
was gone and that he had accepted it, even gotten used to
it. He still had a life to live, a life he wanted to live. And

he wanted to make way for those fresh starts he was ready for.

By the middle of that afternoon Zoey was all set to go to work. Her camera was loaded and ready. She had seen Dillon and Jessy leave around lunchtime, and used the opportunity to go up the hill to judge where best to position herself so as not to be spotted while she took her pictures. Then she had gathered all she needed under the trampoline, including a pillow on which to sit for the hours she expected to keep watch through the window that rose up above a camouflaging hedge.

Everything was ready. Dillon and Jessy had come home. Jessy had gone down for a nap.

That had been over an hour ago and Zoey assumed the little girl would be getting up anytime now. She knew she should get into position and be prepared to start taking those pictures. But somehow Zoey couldn't make herself move off the sofa. This was not a job that sat well on her conscience. In fact, she felt as if she were betraying a trust.

It wasn't as if they were really friends, she told herself for the fourth time in as many hours. Or as if Dillon had placed any trust in her. But still she couldn't shake the feeling.

"Admit it. You like the man," she told herself. But even as she said it she knew that liking him was only the tip of the iceberg.

Okay, so maybe she was in lust with the guy. But she knew that lust wasn't much more than the second tip of the iceberg.

The truth was that there was more to this attraction. There was what he stirred inside of her. Things that hadn't been alive for a long while. For eight and a half years.

Carl had been a very intense, serious man. They'd had the common interest of photography. They'd had stimulating philosophical discussions. They'd had an exciting life living and working together in Africa. Being with him had

made Zoey feel special, intelligent, talented. It had made
her feel chosen. Things she hadn't felt growing up in a
family with eleven kids.

But there had been a trade-off. There wasn't much light-
heartedness or teasing or humor in their relationship. It just
hadn't been in Carl's nature. So Zoey had suppressed that
side of herself. She had been what Carl wanted her to be.
Done only what Carl wanted her to do. Behaved only the
way Carl wanted her to behave.

But she had missed that lighter side of her own nature
more and more as time went by. She had even worried after
Carl died if she would ever be able to find it in herself
again. But as if it had never left, here it was, bursting to
the surface every time she'd been with Dillon Mills. And
it felt good.

Did he deserve to be repaid for bringing that part of her
back to life by being spied on? she had to ask herself.

He didn't.

But what if what Harold Miflin had alluded to was true?
the argument went. What if Dillon was an unfit father?
Should Jessy be left with him just because he had made
Zoey laugh and feel good and carefree again? Should the
little girl be taken away from people who had already been
awarded guardianship of her and done the good job Zoey
had mistakenly attributed to Dillon?

But that was the point, wasn't it? The decision needed
to be made as to who was best to raise Jessy. And her
pictures were aimed at swaying that decision one way or
another. She wasn't personally involved with Dillon. She
didn't want to be. She needed to remember that. And Jessy
needed to be raised by whomever was best for the job.

Zoey took a deep breath and pushed herself off the
couch. "So, go to work," she said.

And if her tone was tinged with a trace of self-loathing,
it was just something she'd have to live with.

Zoey's phone rang at five that afternoon. It didn't take a
genius to assume the call was from Dillon since she had

watched him come into his kitchen, pick up the phone and dial. It also didn't take her more than two rings to decide to answer it.

"I've done a terrible thing, and if you want me shot at dawn I won't blame you," he said to her hello.

The sound of his deep voice sent a little shiver through her at the same moment her conscience pricked. "I can't believe you've done anything that bad," she said, thinking, *in comparison to what you've been accused of and what I'm up to.*

"Better reserve judgment until you hear."

"I'm all ears."

"I bribed my daughter not to wet her pants and she's stayed dry as a bone."

"Not so bad. Now you'll just have to pay up."

"That's the problem. She wanted it worth her while, so the only thing she'd agree to was jumping on your tramp."

Busy place, that tramp. "I see," she mused. But before she could say any more, he went on.

"So, if I bring burgers and fries down there for the three of us for dinner, do you think that could be arranged?"

"You don't need to do that," she said in a hurry. She'd been thinking of where to escape to while he was here.

"I want to. It's the least I can do after bartering with something that wasn't mine. And then you can see that I do sometimes make my daughter eat a square meal."

"You consider hamburgers and fries a square meal?" It had sounded as if he was teasing about that part, but now Zoey couldn't be sure. And she was torn. On the one hand his charm was magnetic. On the other, he had been found unfit as a father.

"How about *sort of* a square meal? So what do you say?"

"I was going to run to the store," she lied. "Why don't you come down and let her jump while I'm gone. You really don't have to feed me as payment."

"You think I'm a moocher?" he joked. "If you don't let me feed you, I'll feel rotten about this."

And if she fraternized with him she'd feel rotten. Wouldn't she? Wasn't it bad enough to spy on him from a distance? How could she compound her deceit by spending time with him? By getting to know him any more than she already had?

"Don't tell me," he said a little more seriously. "Yesterday was enough with some guy and his two-and-a-half-year-old terror."

"No, it isn't that at all," she denied quickly. Harold Miflin's words about stacking the deck against Dillon rang in her mind. It occurred to her that maybe getting to know him was just what she should do. After all, what better way to judge for herself what kind of person and parent he was? She didn't want her pictures unconsciously slanted against him just because the accusations had been leveled and she had seen a few things that might make them seem valid. Didn't she owe him a chance to disprove these allegations against him?

"Can you give me half an hour?" she said.

"You're sure?"

"Positive." And much, much too anxious.

"Great. We'll be down in half an hour, then." He paused a minute before saying in a tone of voice that wasn't teasing at all, "You know this was a ploy, don't you? You were on my mind all day and I really just wanted to see you again."

What to say to that? "Oh, sure. You're just trying to cover up bartering my tramp," she said, making a joke and wishing her heart wasn't pounding a pleased response to his admission.

"Well, I don't want to be shot at dawn, now, do I?" His voice was rich and wonderful.

"Half an hour, Mills," she clipped out, trying to suppress her appreciation.

He chuckled. "Half an hour, Carmichael."

* * *

For that half hour Zoey flew around her house, taking all of her equipment out from under the tramp, changing her clothes, combing her hair, glossing her lips and finally mixing a salad and heating a can of green beans.

The sound of Jessy's voice squealing in delight announced Dillon at her back door.

"Hi, Zowy. I'm down here. I'm superguy," the little girl said. Standing on the patio, Dillon acted as if he wasn't even aware that he was carrying Jessy upside down, holding her feet up to his ears. He stepped inside, handed Zoey the hamburger bag and flipped his daughter over onto the floor. Then he grinned at Zoey.

"What did you do around here all day long, Carmichael? The place looks the same as it did yesterday and the day before that."

I wrestled with my conscience is what, she thought. But instead she pretended effrontery. "I beg your pardon. I'll have you know that I emptied two full boxes."

"Ah, how could I have missed it." He took Jessy's hand and the bag back from Zoey, and headed toward the table as if he was right at home. "What's all this?" he asked, referring to the place settings, the salad and green beans.

"A square meal," she informed.

Zoey held out the chair on which she'd stacked phone books and Dillon lifted Jessy onto them. Then Zoey tied a dish towel around her and the ladder-back in lieu of a high chair.

"You do have some experience at this kid stuff, don't you?" he observed as he passed out hamburgers and fries.

"A little," she answered wryly.

"I hate burglars," Jessy informed her father as he set the food down in front of her. "I wan sherries and socolate."

"You can't have cherries and chocolate. And if you want to jump on the tramp, you have to eat what's in front of you."

Jessy made a face.

Dillon dipped a fry in ketchup and held it out to her. "How about this?"

Jessy squinted her eyes and turned to Zoey. "I doan like when he does that."

From there Jessy let it be known she preferred jumping on the trampoline to eating dinner. Zoey ate in near silence while Dillon coerced his daughter through every bite of burger and fries, having no luck at all with the salad or green beans.

"I wanna jup now," she said sweetly, changing tactics when about half of her dinner was gone. "Please, Dad, dear?" Her cherubic face was all sublime innocence, her eyes wide, and a deliciously mischievous smile tugged at her mouth.

Zoey knew before he said anything that this would be Dillon's undoing.

"I give up," he said.

Zoey burst out laughing. "I knew you would."

He grinned at her. "Okay. So I'm a sucker." He took the last of his own hamburger along with him and put Jessy on the tramp.

"They don't call these the 'terrible twos' for nothing," Zoey told him as she cleared the table. Once again impressed by his patience when another man might have lost his temper, she wondered how that fit in with the bad-dad accusation. She put the few dishes into the dishwasher and then joined him at the side of the tramp, noting that he was careful about Jessy's safety.

"Well, I had a productive day," he said.

"Oh?" she answered simply, because it seemed like a segue. He had a fresh-scrubbed look about him, as if he had showered just before coming down. His red polo shirt and khaki slacks were clean and unwrinkled and his loafers were polished to a gleam.

"I cleaned out Linda's closet."

"Oh." Zoey didn't know what to say to that. All she could think was why had it taken him so long?

"I know," he said as if reading her thoughts. "I've been putting it off."

"It isn't an easy thing to do."

"Actually, maybe waiting is the best way. It wasn't fun, but it wasn't a gut-wrencher, either."

"Mmm. A gut-wrencher is just what it is when you do it early on."

"Is that what you did?"

"Everything seemed like a reminder and I thought it would help to have them gone."

"It didn't?"

She shook her head. "Grief has its own timetable."

He agreed with a nod. "Did you feel guilty?"

"For getting rid of Carl's belongings? Yes, tremendously. It was almost as if I thought he'd come back the next day and find out what I'd done."

Dillon chuckled. "It felt disloyal to me, too. Of course I was thinking about someone else along the way, and that didn't help my conscience any. Even though after two years I'm entitled."

Since he had already told her on the phone that he had been thinking about her all day, it wasn't hard for her to guess who had been on his mind. "After Carl's death," she said, rather than acknowledging what he had hinted at, "I didn't know which end was up." She glanced at him. He was smiling kindly, his expression showing an understanding no one who hadn't gone through the experience could have.

"Shock," he named it. "And then trying to comprehend the incomprehensible."

"Mmm. That's just what it was—incomprehensible. There isn't a gradual disintegration of the marriage to look back on and analyze, the way there is in a divorce. An illness might have warned you but with accidents, one day they're there and the next they aren't. There's nothing to help you understand or grasp what's happened."

"Did you have much support, being in Africa?"

"I had a few close friends, but I missed my family something fierce, then. Did you?"

"I only have my brother and his wife, but they were great. I couldn't have made it without them. They live not far from here."

The conversation stalled for a moment. They both watched Jessy jumping uninhibitedly. Then Zoey said, "It must have been hard being left with a small baby."

"Not nearly as hard as the loss."

Did he mean the loss of his wife, or the loss of Jessy to his in-laws? she wondered. But of course she couldn't ask that. "It's amazing how you do heal, though," she said instead.

"Even though sometimes you aren't sure you'll be able to. Then there's that first time you realize you're enjoying yourself at something and you feel guilty as hell because there you are, not only going on living but laughing, too, when that person you loved is gone."

"I thought I was the only one to feel like that."

"No, it hit me, too." His eyes were still on her, exuding a warmth that left her speechless. "Well, this is cheery after-dinner conversation, isn't it?" he said with a laugh.

She glanced at Jessy again and admitted, "Not cheery, but it's nice to find out what I went through was normal."

"I understand that."

Silence fell again for a moment. Then Zoey spoke, changing the subject. "How long have you lived here?"

"Ten years."

"That's strange. Saturday, when I first found Jessy, I took her around to the neighbors to see if anyone knew who she was. No one did." Okay, so she was fishing. She just wished there was a way to get him to tell her about the custody case. She couldn't help hoping he could defend himself, that he could give her reason to believe he was what he seemed and not what he'd been accused of.

But all he said was, "I keep to myself. And I can't say

I've been around much in the past two years. But things are going to change.''

Did those changes include his method of parenting? ''How?'' she asked.

Dillon shrugged. ''Oh, a lot of ways. For one I've come to the conclusion that it's time to go on with other relationships.''

It was clear by the direct look of his warm blue eyes that he was talking about her. Zoey knew she shouldn't be feeling the pleasure she was, but sharing such personal parts of their pasts and their grief seemed to have formed the tenuous beginnings of a bond between them, on top of confirming all over again how much she liked this man, how comfortable she felt with him, how easy it was for her to confide in him. All together they were feelings she couldn't resist at that moment.

She looked up into that chiseled face of his and all she could do was nod once. Yet when she had, she wasn't sure whether it was a nod of understanding or consent.

Holding her eyes with his, he reached a finger to her temple, smoothing it down the side of her face in a feathery touch that lit sparks along the way. Then he bent slightly forward and kissed her, a bare touch of his lips to hers. Once. Twice.

The third time he came a little more firmly and stayed slightly longer, wrapping her in the clean scent of his aftershave before leaving her again.

And then on the fourth his mouth took her completely. Warm and wonderful, his lips parted, inviting but not demanding. It was so nice that Zoey answered the invitation by letting her own mouth relax, her lips ease slowly apart, her head tilt farther back.

She hadn't realized until that moment how much she had missed being kissed, missed the feel of a man's mouth on hers. She felt his hands move to her elbows, pulling her gently toward him. In her mind she finished the path before he did, imagining those powerful arms all the way around her, those big hands pressing her back, the feel of her breasts against that muscled chest.

And then, like a flash, she remembered the job she had accepted just this morning. She remembered the accusations against this man. She remembered that she didn't want any serious involvement with any man.

And she stopped.

"That hamburger was heady stuff," she said shakily, trying for levity and failing.

For a moment Dillon studied her, and she was grateful that nowhere in his expression did she read rejection. Then he smiled in that slow, kind way he had that made her feel so good, so understood and accepted. "It all went to your head and left you with cold feet," he guessed.

No that wasn't the problem. Nothing about her was cold. She was all too warm and wanting more of what she had just ended. But rather than answer him, she glanced at Jessy and took the coward's way out. "Careful, Jessy. Don't get too near that other side."

She heard Dillon chuckle, a low, throaty, sexy rumble, and she could feel his gaze on her a moment more. Then he said, "Come on, Jess. It's past your bedtime."

The difference in his tone of voice when he spoke to his daughter and what it had been in these past few minutes was remarkable. Yet she hadn't realized until that moment just how far into intimacy he'd gone even before the kiss.

Jessy put up a fight against ending her evening and the sound of her "No way. Doan wanna go to bed tonight," reassured Zoey that they were back on safe, firm ground.

Dillon reached across the tramp and caught his daughter. "You can come back another time," he promised as he lifted her to his hip. The child stuck her thumb in her mouth in unwilling acceptance and dropped her forehead to his cheek.

"Thanks for bailing me out," Dillon said then. "The rest of my week is tied up with Jessy, but I'd like to see you on Saturday. Think we could arrange it?"

Too tempting. Zoey seized suspicion as a way out. "Where will Jessy be on Saturday?"

"With her grandparents," he answered simply.

If only the evening hadn't been so good, she thought. If only it hadn't been so nice to talk to someone who understood what she'd been through in the past eighteen months. "Saturday sounds good," she heard herself say out of the blue, before she'd even realized she was going to agree.

"Great. I'll call you." He dipped in for another kiss. It was brief and chaste, but goose bumps erupted over her skin, all the same. And then he was gone.

Zoey closed her eyes. *Idiot. Fool. Jerk. Dummy. What did you do?* She wished she could call back the agreement. But *you're glad you can't,* a little voice in the back of her mind whispered.

"You're not too smart, you know it, Carmichael?" she said to herself. But smart or not, there was something happening between her and Dillon Mills. There was heat.

"First you'll spend your week spying on him, then you'll go out with him on Saturday?"

It occurred to her that maybe, just maybe, after a week of spying on him she'd know for sure that he wasn't a negligent, unfit father. And then they could be friends, after all.

Friends. Just friends, she reassured herself.

Fat chance, whispered that little voice.

Chapter Five

The week passed too fast and the knot was back in Dillon's gut. It was with him Saturday morning, when he woke up earlier than his dawn-rising daughter.

Staying in bed, he listened for sounds of her and mentally shored himself up for bringing her back to the Whites. At least it would only be for a few days, he thought. The court date was set for Wednesday. After that this whole mess would be behind him. Jessy would be home for good.

But the knot didn't go away.

As confident as he was that his daughter would be given back to him, he knew nothing was ever certain. That the judge could have beliefs as antiquated as the Whites', was one of the scenarios that haunted him at weak moments. But luckily those moments were rare.

This morning's knot, he decided, was just impatience to have this over with, and understandable reluctance to bring his daughter back to her grandparents. Only a few more days, he told himself again and got out of bed.

The house was dark and cool in the early hour, but Dillon didn't have the sense of it being big and empty the way he did most mornings. Jessy wasn't a large presence, but still just knowing she was there seemed to fill the place, give it a purpose.

He went silently into her room to check on her. She was still sleeping peacefully, her thumb in her mouth, her other arm around a ragged dog, and her fingers rubbing a satin lop ear. Murph was the dog's name. Dillon didn't know where the toy and name had come from, and that lack of knowledge stabbed him.

Two years was too much time to have been a long-distance father. Especially since Jessy had lived only two and a half.

Dillon crossed his forearms on the top of the crib rail and bent over to rest his chin on them. She sighed and turned away from him, leaving her rump up in the air in his direction. It made Dillon smile and want to pat it. But if he did he'd wake her, and so he refrained. Instead he straightened and glanced out the window at the sun just beginning to rise in a haze of persimmon.

From there his gaze wandered down to Zoey's house much the way it had a thousand times during this past week. The temptation to call her had been tremendous. So tremendous, in fact, that had it ever seemed that she was at home he might not have been able to resist. But there hadn't been a sign of her, at all, so he had stuck to his resolve to concentrate solely on Jessy. But it hadn't been easy.

In a perfect world he wouldn't have to worry about an idiotic custody suit or have to be overly cautious about sharing his time with both his daughter and a woman. The three of them could have more times like Sunday at the zoo, or Monday night at Zoey's. He definitely wanted more times like those, along with some alone with Zoey.

Only a few more days, he reminded himself yet again. He'd have this weekend alone with Zoey, then the court hearing would be over with, and by next weekend the three of them could see each other without his worrying about it.

"Dad, gimme up," Jessy said from behind him just then.

It was weird how powerful that little voice calling him dad was. Dillon turned from staring at Zoey's dark house to smile at his daughter. "Good morning, lazy bones," he said as he went back to her where she stood in the crib now.

"Kin we have doughnuts and foffee?" she asked sweetly, holding her arms out to him.

"Doughnuts and coffee, huh?" He picked her up. Feeling her chunky feet cold against his bare belly, he took them in his free hand to warm them. "Ooh, cold toes, Jess. How about a nice warm bath first? Then we'll buy your doughnuts and go wake up Uncle Frank to see what he wanted when he left that message on the machine last night?"

"Doan wan no bath. I wan doughnuts and foffee," Jessy answered.

Dillon laughed. "First the bath. Then the doughnuts."

It was seven-thirty when Dillon pulled up at the curb in front of his brother's trilevel house. But the morning paper was nowhere in sight, so he assumed someone was up. Taking Jessy and the box of doughnuts, he went to the front door where he could hear the sound of the television.

"Push the doorbell," he told Jessy, who was more than willing.

Seconds later his ten-year-old niece, wearing pajamas, opened it. "Hi, Uncle D," she said as she let him in.

"Anybody up but you?"

"Mom and Dad are in the kitchen, but Cathy is still asleep. She was at the mall last night and she says she's sleeping till noon today," Erika informed him, rolling her eyes and lending ample exaggeration to the word mall to make fun of her fourteen-year-old sister's entertainments. "Hi, Jess. Want to watch cartoons with me?"

"Wanna doughnut?" Jessy offered instead.

Dillon put his daughter down and headed through the connecting dining room toward the kitchen. "Come in here and we'll break them out."

"Doan break 'em," Jessy complained, following behind.

"Here I thought I was going to get to roust you out of bed," Dillon greeted his brother and sister-in-law. "I tried calling you back until late last night but there was no answer, so Jess and I decided to come in person."

Frank's blond hair was tousled and he was wearing a bathrobe over boxer shorts, his feet up on a kitchen chair and the morning paper in his lap. "Blame it on Sharon. She forced me to a neighbor's party against my will and then held me hostage there till after midnight."

"Some hostage," blond, blue-eyed Sharon put in from over a cup of coffee. "First he was shooting hoops in the driveway with their teenage son, and then I couldn't get him away from swapping fishing stories with one of the other guests."

Dillon pushed his brother's feet off the chair and sat down. "Well, I'll share my doughnuts, if you'll share your coffee."

"Erika, pour your uncle a cup," Frank told his daughter over his shoulder. "Then you can put some doughnuts in a dish and take Jess out to eat them in front of the TV."

Not a good sign, Dillon knew. He had been hoping Frank's call had been just to talk or invite him to dinner or something harmless. But if the kids needed to be out of earshot that couldn't be the case. "Thanks, skinny," he said to Erika when she delivered the coffee. All three adults watched silently as the kids took what they wanted and left the kitchen. "What's up?" Dillon asked the minute they were gone.

Frank tipped his chair back on two legs. "The court date's been postponed."

Dillon's cup stopped halfway to his mouth and the knot in his stomach clenched. "Why?"

Frank shrugged.

"Could last Saturday's fiasco with the police have anything to do with it?" Dillon wondered aloud.

But Frank only shrugged again. "There's nothing going on that I don't know about, is there?"

"You mean besides the orgies in the attic and all those times I ran naked to the mailbox?"

"Yeah, besides those. Look, I still don't think there's anything to worry about. Even if they do have the police report."

"I'm not as worried as I am tired of waiting. They could put this off until Jessy's eighteen, and then it won't make much difference, will it?"

"It's not a long delay. They've pushed it back to a week from Monday," Frank said. "I'm sorry, man. But it's all going to come out in the wash. You'll see."

"It really will," Sharon put in. "Another week isn't such a long time. You said you wanted to get the crib taken down and buy Jessy a real bed. Use the time for that. I'll go shopping with you and help pick it out, if you want."

Dillon swallowed his anger. It wasn't at Frank and Sharon, and of all people, they were the last two who deserved it. He owed them both too much to take it out on them.

"Want to go blow off some steam shooting baskets? The guy from last night said I could come up and use his hoop whenever I wanted."

Dillon conceded to a smile at that, albeit a weak one. "I have you by four inches, Frank. You never could take me at basketball."

"I was hot last night."

Now Dillon's grin was genuine, as he winked at Sharon. "Is that true?"

"Don't believe it," she said.

Dillon answered his brother's invitation, then. "I can't. I still have to pack Jess's things and then I have a date."

"Let me guess. The neighbor from down the hill," Frank said slyly.

"Give the man two points." Dillon finished his coffee and took his cup to the sink.

"Actually, having the hearing postponed is a good deal. Maybe you can get married by then, after all, huh?" Frank teased.

"Not before we get to meet her," Sharon chided.

"Today will be the first time I've seen this lady without my small chaperon, guys. I could be wrong, but I think marriage is a little way off, yet." He went into the living room and scooped up Jessy.

"Well, work on that, would you?" Frank said as he followed.

"Right," Dillon answered sarcastically as he went out the door.

"We'll be here all day and night, if you want to stop by," Sharon called from behind her husband's back as Dillon buckled Jessy into the car seat.

"I'll keep it in mind," he said over the roof and then got in behind the wheel and started the car. After one last wave, Dillon pulled away from the curb. He sighed again, this time resolutely. Another week's delay. Dammit.

But somehow the lingering thought of Zoey took part of the sting out. It surprised him to find how strong her effect on him was. But he didn't question it. Seeing her again, getting to know her better, put a new spin on passing the time until this custody business was over with. And anything that helped was too good to wonder about.

Zoey went to the phone with every intention of calling her sister. But instead she pushed the play button on the answering machine beside it. This was the eighth time she'd listened to Dillon's voice calling the night before to confirm their date today. He would come around and pick her up at noon. He hoped she didn't mind dropping Jessy off at her grandparents' house first. Then, since that was in Boulder, he thought they'd have lunch and spend the afternoon browsing around Boulder's downtown mall.

But instead of dialing Jane's number when the message was finished, Zoey wandered to her back door and stared up at the house on the hill, one of the few times since Monday that she'd done so without being camouflaged or behind a camera.

A full week and two dozen rolls of film, and she still couldn't make up her mind about what kind of a father Dillon was.

Standing there watching Arachnid snooze in the dog run, Zoey thought about those pictures she'd taken. Some of them showed Dillon as a model dad—reading Jessy bedtime stories, playing with her, showing her how to make sand sculptures, tickling her, giving her rides on his back while he was down on all fours. There was even one Zoey particularly liked of Dillon rocking her to sleep in the chair in the nursery.

But other pictures didn't look so great. There was a shot through Jessy's bedroom door of her hanging precariously from the balusters at the top of the staircase before Dillon discovered her and took her down. There were two of Jessy climbing from a chair onto a kitchen counter and taking a knife from a wooden block. There was Jessy, again after having used a chair to climb, trying to recapture a balloon string by standing on top of the very edge of the kitchen table. There was Jessy dipping a finger in the scouring cleanser to taste it. There was Jessy playing in and eating out of the kitchen trash. There was Jessy nose to nose with Arachnid, the little girl bending far back as if in fear of the alarmingly dangerous-looking animal. There was Jessy climbing the changing table and pulling the whole thing over on top of her. All with Dillon nowhere in sight.

So far, through Zoey's viewfinder, Jessy seemed to have come out relatively unscathed and Dillon seemed calm enough. But watching left Zoey a nervous wreck. Her whole week had been torn between worrying about how those pictures might influence a judge and worrying about Jessy. Twice Zoey had taken the shot, dropped the camera and run halfway up the hill to rescue the little girl herself before Dillon had reappeared and Zoey had gone back into hiding to shoot more pictures.

"Why can't things just be clearly black or white?" she said aloud.

How much easier it would have been to believe Dillon was neglectful if he left Jessy alone while he drove off somewhere, or if he didn't bother to feed her at all, or if any one of a dozen other overtly bad things happened. But that wasn't the case.

On the other hand, there wasn't a doubt in Zoey's mind that a small child needed closer supervision, more precautionary measures and fewer hazards she could get to. Zoey just plain couldn't deny that some of those pictures made her cringe. But the bottom line was that she didn't have any better idea now than before of whether Dillon was actually unfit to have custody of his daughter.

Zoey spun away from the door. She picked up the phone and punched her sister's number. "Hi, it's me," she said when Jane answered.

"My sister the undercover agent?" Jane teased. Zoey had talked to her several times during the week, and her sister was well aware of the job she had taken on, as well as Zoey's mixed feelings.

"I called to ask a favor," Zoey said seriously.

"Shoot."

"If I decide to keep this date with Dillon, can I trump up some reason and bring him to your house?"

"Sure," Jane agreed, but there was a question in her tone.

"I want you to get into a conversation with him about how little kids need to be watched every minute," Zoey explained. "Tim isn't too much older than Jessy, so you'll seem like an expert. Maybe he just doesn't know what he's supposed to do. I mean, think of Dad. If he'd ever been left alone with one of us, he wouldn't have had the foggiest idea.''

Jane didn't say anything for a moment, but her silence was disapproving. "If this man really is neglectful it isn't something you can fix, Zoey."

"I know that. But somebody else cast the shadow of doubt and I feel like I should give him the benefit of one. The time frame of all of this makes me wonder. His wife died two years ago. That was when Jessy was taken away from him and it was the beginning of the gap in his work projects. That can't be a coincidence. Maybe his wife's death hit him really hard and he had some sort of breakdown or something?''

"And abused his daughter in the process? Even if that was true, would you feel comfortable giving her back to him—knowing it had happened once, and seeing that he isn't the perfect dad, even now?''

Zoey couldn't refute that. "I just think maybe a little instruction on how to be a superparent can't hurt anything.''

"Okay, kiddo," Jane said dubiously. "Bring him over. I'll even set my mothers' manuals out on the coffee table, if you think it'll help.''

When Zoey hung up she couldn't resist listening to Dillon's message one more time. How could a voice that sounded so rich and nice and considerate come from an unfit father?

"You just don't want to believe it," she said to herself, knowing that the sound of somebody's voice didn't prove anything. Except maybe that she was very, very susceptible to the man.

No matter how many times she reminded herself that she didn't want to be involved with him, there were certain parts of what she had spied on this past week that she had enjoyed. A little too much. Having him in her viewfinder hour after hour had not been a hardship by any means. And whether she wanted to admit it or not, the urge to see him again was overwhelming.

Was that why she felt inclined to give him the benefit of the doubt? Because she was so attracted to him?

It was possible.

But wasn't what she had suggested to Jane possible, too? Couldn't there have been extenuating circumstances that caused him to lose Jessy in the first place? Wasn't it possible that now simple inexperience and oversight made him look like a bad father?

She was grasping at straws, she knew. Something pretty awful had to have happened to make the courts take a child away from her father and place her with grandparents.

But still Zoey held onto a thread of hope. And maybe if she spent time with him, asked questions and he opened up to her, she'd have a better idea of what was really going on with Dillon and Jessy. Of what had happened in those two years since his wife died.

Zoey had invaded his privacy, now she felt she owed him a chance to explain—even if he didn't know he was explaining anything. Then she could judge. Because finding out just what kind of man he really was had suddenly become very personal to her. And until she was satisfied one way or the other, she knew she wouldn't be able to rest.

She went into the bedroom section of the house and took out her good jeans and a crisp white tank top.

"Okay, Dillon," she said as she got dressed. "Today at noon."

The drive to Boulder passed in a bevy of "What's that?" chatter from Jessy. Zoey answered the little girl most of the way, since Dillon seemed unusually quiet and preoccupied.

It wasn't easy for him to bring the little girl back to her grandparents, Zoey thought, and so she put extra effort into entertaining Jessy and leaving him to drive and deal with whatever was going on in his mind.

The Whites' house was on the northernmost side of Boulder, a huge three-story brick Georgian structure set so far back from the road that it was barely visible when they first passed through the iron gates that secured it.

"All set, Jess?" Dillon asked when he had stopped the car in the circle drive out front.

"No," the little girl said forcefully. "I doan wanna."

"I'm sorry, sweetheart, but you have to."

"Yur mean at me," Jessy accused.

Zoey saw strain tighten Dillon's features, and her heart went out to him. She didn't know what to do and so left Jessy and her outthrust bottom lip to him. But through the tinted windows of his car she watched them all the way to the front landing where Dillon rang the bell.

A woman in a maid's uniform opened the left side of the double doorway. Her expression was blank as she accepted Jessy's suitcase and then reached for the little girl.

Zoey heard Jessy's "No!" all the way out in the driveway and saw the child cling tenaciously to her father's neck. The maid took hold of her and Dillon had to pry his daughter's arms away. When he leaned to give her a kiss she tried to grab him again but he eluded her grasp. Then the maid stepped back into the house and closed the door.

For a moment Dillon just stood there, his back ramrod-straight. He jammed his hands into the back pockets of his jeans as if to keep himself from pounding on that closed door and grabbing his daughter back. Zoey couldn't help feeling that seeing him like this was more of an intrusion than the whole week of taking pictures.

She looked away, picking up her purse to rummage inside. It must not have fooled Dillon because moments later when he got in the car he said "Separation anxiety," as if to explain what had happened at the door, leaving Zoey wondering whether he meant his own or Jessy's.

Zoey had the overpowering urge to touch him, to reach

out to him, and that was just what she did. For only a moment, she squeezed his arm.

He covered her hand with his, patting it appreciatively. But he didn't seem to want to talk about what was going on with him. Instead he said, "Are you ready to crawl the mall?"

"I thought the mall crawl was only on Halloween night. But I'm ready if you are. I haven't been to Boulder since before I got married."

He started the car and Zoey watched his gaze catch on the house for a moment as they pulled away. But then he glanced at her. "Well, it hasn't changed much."

For the second time she wasn't sure exactly what he meant. Was it the outdoor mall and Boulder that hadn't changed? Or was it the Whites' house and his reception there? But of course she didn't ask. Instead she let the silence hang between them, not knowing what else to do for this man who stirred more and more of her curiosity as well as her senses.

Classical flute, African drums, jazz trumpet, guitar and singing—good and bad—provided some of the sidewalk entertainment along Boulder's cobbled outdoor mall. There were also two balloon sculptors, a one-man band, an accordionist, four jugglers, a magician and several people passing out pamphlets for their own particular causes. A man in a top hat and long black cape performed Shakespeare while two recited their own poetry. A bedraggled-looking man with a scraggly beard and mustache, stood with his hat out on the walkway for coins, like all the rest, but it was impossible to tell whether he was reciting, lecturing or merely wanted to be paid for talking to himself.

Among the people out to watch all of this in between shopping in the specialty stores were an assortment of flower children who looked as if no one had told them the sixties were over, a group of college students in togas, leather-jacketed teenagers in various arrays of spiked hair

or shaved heads—the best being a girl whose entire head
was bald except for a single foot-long horn of hair sticking
out in front like a unicorn—and a fair share of well dressed,
upscale-looking folks just to balance out the weirdness. If
Dillon had been talking about Boulder, he'd been right—it
hadn't changed.

Lunch was hot dogs from a vendor, but for dinner Dillon
insisted he take Zoey to the Morgul Bismarck Saloon, an
art-deco restaurant on Pearl Street that was packed to the
rafters. The fresh tomato pizza and vegetables dipped in
balsamic vinegar were wonderful, but like the rest of the
afternoon, conversation centered around the sights and
sounds and food rather than anything personal. It wasn't
until they got into the car to go back to Denver that Zoey
felt as if she and Dillon were actually alone.

"Would you mind stopping at my sister Jane's house?
It's not far from where we live. I have to drop off last
week's wedding pictures for her to relay or I'm going to
be in big trouble," Zoey said, when they had pulled out of
the parking lot.

"No problem. Just direct me when we get near."

The somberness of Dillon's earlier mood had eased and
the good-spirited, easy nature that so appealed to Zoey had
returned. She had enjoyed this day. Maybe too much, because she had never gotten around to the subject she had
set out to explore.

"So, where were you all week long?" he asked before
she could think of a segue.

"All week?" she repeated with too much innocence,
taken off guard by the question and the instant response of
her guilty conscience.

"It was late every night before I saw a light on in your
place and I didn't see you outside once."

"Watching, were you?" she teased to buy time.

He grinned. "Every now and then. But it was pretty un-
satisfying."

"I was just busy," she answered enigmatically. And actually it was the truth. Besides her mission as a spy, she had used all those sleepless nights to finish unpacking boxes and settle into her house. "How about you? What was your week like?"

"Busy, too. Jessy is a handful. I don't know how anyone could do it with eleven." He paused a moment. "How was it growing up with that many brothers and sisters?"

Zoey shrugged. "Good and bad, like everything."

"Did you ever wish to be an only child?"

"Like Jessy?" She laughed. "A million times."

"I don't think it's all that great. In fact I don't want Jessy to be an only child forever."

"I'd think having more kids would be the last thing on your mind right now." The words came out before she remembered she wasn't supposed to know about the custody suit.

Luckily, Dillon misunderstood. "Being unmarried does complicate it," he agreed.

"But you do want more kids?" she fished.

"Not ten," he teased. "But, yeah, one or two more. Like I said, I don't want to raise Jess by herself."

If he had doubts about winning custody they didn't sound in his voice. Was it confidence? Or was he just camouflaging? After all, who would want it known he'd been accused of being an unfit parent? And yet, if anything, her afternoon with Dillon only confirmed her earlier opinion of him as a nice guy.

"What about you?" he interrupted her thoughts. "Seven years married but no kids—how come?"

Zoey shrugged. "Carl didn't want any. He planned to spend his life traveling—New Zealand, South America, the North Pole. A child didn't fit into that."

"What about you? Didn't you want kids?"

"Until I met Carl I saw them in my future, yes," she said, surprised at the softness and regret that echoed in her own tone. She'd thought she had put that behind her long ago.

"But you gave that up for him?" Dillon said, with a trace of amazement.

Zoey laughed wryly. "He came first."

"And by the sound of your voice, it isn't something you'd repeat if you had it to do over again."

The man was perceptive, too. Or was she just that transparent? "No, I wouldn't do it again," she admitted. "It isn't that I didn't love Carl. I did. And even though he expected to come first, I did it willingly. But after a while…well, let's just say being responsible only for myself and getting my business back in gear is enough."

Dillon took his eyes off the road for a moment and glanced at her. "I can understand loving your husband and still not wanting to have the same kind of marriage you had with him. I think we all grow and change as we get older. We gain some experience, we get to know ourselves better. As much as I loved Linda, she isn't what I want the second time around, either. Her life centered on our home and family, which was great at the time. But now, having someone who has interests of her own, goals of her own, is what I'd rather have in my life."

There seemed to be an underlying message to what he said. Zoey was hesitant to explore it. "Turn left at the next light," she instructed instead and then changed the subject. "Jane has a three-year-old son. The two of you ought to have a lot to talk about."

"Where in the birth order does Jane come?" he asked after a moment, obviously conceding to her need to talk about something else.

"She's next down, not quite two years younger than me. It's that red-brick on the right. Her little boy's name is Tim. Jane is a great mom." Now she did feel transparent. She curbed the urge to go into accolades about what a terrific parent her sister was. "You can park in the driveway."

"There aren't any lights on in the house," Dillon observed as he turned the car off.

"The kitchen is in back. Maybe she's there. I told her I was coming."

But there was no sign of a light from the rear of the house, either, and no one answered when Zoey rang the bell, knocked or called through the living-room window.

"I don't understand. Jane is so conscientious."

"You could just leave the pictures in the mailbox," Dillon suggested.

Since Zoey's second round of attempts to raise anyone failed, she didn't have much choice. *Dammit, Jane. When else am I going to get him over here?*

"We could wait," he offered, when she made it obvious how disinclined she was to go.

"You wouldn't mind?" Zoey jumped at the idea.

He grinned down at her. "No, I wouldn't mind."

"We could go around back. There's a porch swing."

He held out his arm. "Lead the way."

The backyard was very dark, lit only by the blue-white glow of the moon. The swing hung from the patio awning on chains and when Zoey sat on it they squeaked softly. The sound paused as Dillon joined her and then began again, making a steady symphony.

The swing wasn't large and rather than taking the other end, Dillon had chosen the middle, putting him very near Zoey. So near, in fact, that she could feel the heat of his jean-clad thigh running the length of her own. Then he stretched his arm along the back of the swing.

"So, tell me," she said in a hurry, hoping to keep her suddenly ignited senses under control. "What is your philosophy as a parent?" Moonlight dusted his face just enough to let her see him smile at that.

"My philosophy as a parent," he repeated, seeming to mull it over. "I never really thought about it. Spare the rod and spoil the child, maybe? Or love conquers all?"

"Or let them eat cake?" Zoey couldn't resist putting in.

Dillon laughed a rich, throaty sound. "You're the only combination photographer-nutritionist I've ever come across. Was there a shortage of food in your childhood, or what?''

"Okay, okay, no more about the benefits of a good diet. Tell me what you did on your hiatus from work." Not too subtle. But Zoey really was at a loss for how to get into this.

"My hiatus from work?" he asked, not understanding.

"The time you took off after your wife's accident," she nudged gently.

"Oh." He laughed a little. "It was just a very unproductive time," he said noncommittally.

Silence. He obviously was not going to say more about it. Feeling desperate for any information that might help, Zoey said suddenly, "Do you need to go back to Boulder to pick Jessy up?"

"She's staying with her grandparents for a while," he answered simply.

"That's nice. It gives you a break."

He smiled down at her. "I had a good time today," he said as if he hadn't heard her. His voice was lower than it had been before, more intimate, and it seemed to skip across her nerve endings like a stone over a still pool.

"So did I," she admitted, conceding defeat as an undisclosed interrogator.

"I had a hard time staying away this past week," he went on, moving his hand to her shoulder.

She'd seen him watching her house frequently, but her conscience had fretted over his knowing what she was doing rather than his thinking about her as persistently as she had been thinking about him. "Why did you stay away, then?" she heard herself asking.

He rubbed her bare upper arm softly. "It's complicated," he answered. Then he pressed his nose into her hair. "You smell so good."

So did he, damn him. "It's just shampoo," she demurred.

"No, I think it's you."

Little sparks were flaring in the pit of her stomach. "I can't imagine where Jane is."

"We can leave, if you're tired of waiting," he offered, angling his head so that his face was in front of hers.

"No, that's okay," she said in a hurry. There was just the hint of a smile playing on his lips. It was nerve-racking to think he was correctly reading the turmoil going on inside of her.

"Do you know what I'd like more than anything right now?" he asked softly.

"To jump in that wading pool?" she said glibly because her own body temperature seemed to have skyrocketed and she could have used a little cooling off.

"No. I don't think there's been a night this week that I've gone to sleep without thinking about kissing you."

Him, too? "Oh?" she said, intending it to be teasing and instead barely sighing it out.

"That hasn't happened to me since I was seventeen."

She understood too well. Right at that moment, she was feeling the same things too strongly to think about anything but her racing pulse, the tingling, yearning sensation all over her skin, the clean scent of him, the warm feel of him so near, the wanting...

And then his mouth came down to hers, slowly, tenderly, tentatively at first. Just the way she had remembered so many times in the past week. He deepened the kiss, parting his lips, taking hers completely.

A full fireworks display came to life inside Zoey as he pulled her toward him and wrapped his arm around her. She slipped her hands up to his chest, feeling the hardness of well-honed muscles beneath her palms. His face was slightly beard-roughened, but she welcomed that sensation.

She was light-headed and floating. How many times had she imagined this while lying alone in her bed this week? How many times had she awakened with the same thoughts, the same curiosity, wondering if having his arms around her would feel as good as it had promised to feel when he had kissed her before? It did. Better. Much better.

Dillon held her closer still, but not as close as Zoey's body cried out for. She raised her hands to his neck, arching her back and pressing her breasts into him. His hair was as silky as it appeared, and she toyed with it where it waved against his collar. Then she found his neck underneath, corded and tight.

Suddenly his tongue teased her lips open just a little wider and came inside to test the tips of her teeth. It had been a long time since she'd played this game of chase and circle but she reveled in it, feeling more alive than she had the first time it had happened to her. Something about this man was magic, washing away old qualms and inhibitions, the last fadings of grief, even the doubts that had dogged her all week.

From his neck she traced the hard ridge of his collarbone while matching him in the game. His hands began to caress her back, moving up to her shoulder blades and then all the way down to the waistband of her jeans. It felt so good to be touched.

Her tank top slid up and the cooler night air brushed her skin. All she could think was that she wanted the feel of his hands there. And then, as if he knew, he slid them underneath to her bare back. Zoey couldn't help the writhing that answered him, or the way her mouth opened even wider under his.

More. How could she want more? But she did. More from him. More of him.

She dragged her hands down his body and found his shirttails. Up inside she went, marveling at the feel of his skin beneath her palms, from the narrowness of his sides to the widening V just below his armpits. She remembered seeing those tufts of wheaten hair before. She wanted to bring her hands forward, to feel his pectorals, but she wasn't that brave. Instead she smoothed her way around to his back, finding the swell of his shoulder blades almost as arousing.

But Dillon didn't seem to have her timidity. He dropped a hand to her waist, then raised it to the lace edging around her top's armhole. He paused there only a moment before dipping his fingers inside and following the path to the side of her breast until the tips of his fingers reached the sensitive outer circle of her nipple.

It wasn't enough. Almost on their own her breasts strained forward, inviting him to what she needed so much at that moment.

And then he was there, the whole of his hand cupping her breast, pulling her bra away to reach that hardened, yearning crest. Zoey felt as if she were going to burst. Oh, how she wanted this man.

A soft moan escaped her throat. Her head fell back, away from his kiss.

Dillon ran his tongue along the soft underside of her chin, down the arch of her throat to the valley, all the while his hand kneaded her breast, teasing, tormenting her nipple, rolling it between his fingers.

"Ah, Zoey," he said in a raspy voice.

She arched her spine as far as possible, surrendering to him, to the wonder of his hands on her skin. It had never been quite this way with Carl....

Carl. And caring for another person. And putting that other person first.

Zoey gasped and swallowed, opening her eyes. "No," she breathed the word.

Only by inches did he stop—taking his hand from underneath her bra, then sliding back around to her side, down to her waist, staying there with only the lightest of touches.

"Zoey?"

"I don't want to do this," she claimed in a rush.

"You don't?" he said in a way that told her he knew better.

"I can't," she amended.

"Okay." His tone, everything about him was patient, kind, accepting this premature ending with more aplomb than Zoey felt.

"I'm sorry."

"Don't be. Maybe we did rush things a little." He let out a small chuckle. "This certainly isn't the place to have started anything."

Zoey straightened away from him. "I don't think Jane is coming home anytime soon. We might as well go."

But rather than standing, he tipped her face up to his. "Relax. It's okay."

She nodded a bit frantically and nearly jumped to her feet, out of reach of that touch that was so intoxicating. It wasn't until she was at the passenger side of his car that she realized how close behind her he was. He reached and opened the door before she could. Zoey got in, wishing that he wasn't being so nice about this at the same time she felt an abiding appreciation for the way he was handling it.

He walked around the front of the car to the driver's side. She welcomed the hum of the motor to fill the silence as she gathered her wits, and blessed Jane for not living more than six blocks away. Before she knew it Dillon had stopped the car at the curb in front of her house and come around to open her door again.

He took her elbow and headed up the walk. "So tell me, have you ever photographed hot-air balloons floating up into the Sunday morning dawn?" he asked as if nothing more than conversation had passed between them tonight.

Zoey was so relieved he wasn't asking her to tell him something more personal that she laughed. "No, can't say that I have."

"Great. Then I have a photo opportunity for you tomorrow morning."

They had reached her front door. Zoey was searching her purse for her keys and finding some of her composure. "Is that so?" she managed to reply easily enough, finally reaching the point where she, too, sounded almost as if the passion on the porch swing had never happened.

"The truth is that for my next project I'm considering a mechanical approximation of a hot-air balloon ride and I need to experience the real thing for myself so I know what I'm doing. Tomorrow is the last day of the festival and I would really like it if you'd go with me and make a day of it."

"I don't think so," she said on instinct, at the same time another part of her was saying: yes, yes, yes.

He smiled down at her and in the porch light it was warm and charming and heart-wrenching. "Would it help if I promise to keep my hands to myself?"

Zoey didn't want to like him so much. She didn't want her feelings for him to get stronger all the time. But she did, and they were.

"I promise. I really do," he said persuasively.

His cheeks creased deeply when he grinned like that, and Zoey got lost in them and forgot everything else. "Well, I did see a report on the festival on the news last night and thought that I'd really like to go. With any luck I might be able to sell a couple of pictures of it."

"Perfect. But I'll have to pick you up at about five."

"In the morning?"

"I'll bring coffee and breakfast to tide us over. Then we can go for brunch afterward," he offered.

"Okay."

"I'll see you at five, then." He kissed her briefly, chastely, managing to ignite the fireworks all over again anyway. They were still going off when he leaned around her and opened the door. "Good night, Zoey," he said in an intimate, familiar tone that kept the flames warm and bright.

No matter how much she reprimanded herself, she still felt disappointed and a little emptier when he'd gone. For a long while, she leaned back against the door, wondering what in the world was happening to her.

And then her phone rang.

The machine answered before she got there and when she realized the caller wasn't Jane as she'd expected, she just stood listening rather than picking it up.

"This is Harold Miflin. Since Jessica is back with her grandparents your assignment is finished. Please call me at home to arrange for delivery of the pictures to me on Monday. My number is…"

He finished and hung up. Zoey stood there staring at the machine. She should have answered, she knew. For that matter, she should pick up that phone right now and call him back.

But she didn't. She couldn't.

Not until she'd had tomorrow.

Chapter Six

The sunrise couldn't have been more beautiful if it had been a special order. The start of the balloon launching was announced by the sounds of burners sucking air as they were lit. Ballasts were jettisoned and into a brilliant orange, salmon and daffodil-yellow sky the balloons floated amidst cheers from onlookers.

Zoey left Dillon watching from the blanket and sipping coffee, to catch the splendor in her viewfinder. She shot rapid-fire pictures of balloons shaped like an enormous dinosaur, a mansion, a clown head, a basketball in a hoop, a thirteen-story-high champagne bottle, a pink elephant, a spaceship, a golf ball, a teddy bear and a cowboy hat. Interspersed were dozens of the usual shaped ones, some in rainbow-bright colors. Others had unicorns, galaxies, bangles and advertisements as decorations.

"Watch out!"

Dillon's warning was a split second too late, as Zoey stepped backward and stumbled over a boulder. But he was at her side, offering a hand before she even knew what had hit her. Glancing up at his face, she found him grinning.

"You do have a tendency to get involved in your work, don't you?" he said.

If he only knew. "I think somebody just put that thing there to trip me. It was a conspiracy." She took his hand and he hoisted her to her feet.

"A conspiracy, huh? Well, then I better not leave you alone down here. You'll have to take the ride in one of these things with me."

"I'm not crazy about heights," she demurred. "Especially when the only thing between me and falling to my death is a wicker basket."

"What? The African lion tamer is scared of a little height? I don't believe it."

"Believe it."

"It'd give you a new angle for your pictures," he baited. "And I'll make them keep the tether line tied, if that would help you feel better."

Zoey looked at the balloons drifting out of her range. She had to admit that in her mind's eye she could see some great shots from up there.

"I can tell you're tempted," he whispered in her ear, his breath warm and coffee-spiced.

"If I fall out I'll never forgive you."

"I'll hang onto you the whole time," he said, taking her hand in both of his.

"But can I trust a man who promises me breakfast and brings peanut-butter-and-jelly sandwiches?" she asked, trying to ignore the little skitter of sparks that went up her arm at his touch.

He winked at her. "No doubt about it."

Dillon pulled her to one of the four balloons offering the experience of a ride to those adventurous enough to want it. Zoey's heart was pounding, her stomach fluttering, but she wasn't sure of the cause. Stepping into a basket that looked more like a giant planter for flowers than a safe carriage for people was certainly not a relaxing proposition. On the other hand, neither was Dillon opening his arms for her to come into.

"You're sure about this?" she asked dubiously.

He nudged the man operating the balloon. "Tell her it's safe."

"Reasonably," the man said with malicious mischief. But he didn't wait for Zoey to change her mind. Instead he dropped the sandbags that weighted the thing and let it float. The unexpected jolt sent Zoey face-first into Dillon's white T-shirt.

"Good catch," the smart-aleck balloonist complimented.

Dillon's arms closed tightly around her, and even though Zoey had regained her balance he showed no signs of letting her go. Not an altogether unappealing thought, she realized.

She tilted her head back far enough to look up into his face. "I can't take pictures this way."

He smiled with only one side of his mouth. "I said I'd hang onto you the whole time. I didn't say how."

"Well, this isn't the way," she bantered.

"I don't know. I thought this was kind of nice."

"But unproductive."

"Perish the thought," he deadpanned. He held her prisoner for another moment before giving a regretful shake of his head and opening his arms enough for her to turn her back to him. Then he closed them again around her waist.

"Thanks," she said over her shoulder, not sure whether she was grateful for his letting her turn or for putting his arms back around her.

He pulled her closer and growled in her ear, "Take your pictures, Carmichael."

They were up there for over an hour and as time went by Zoey forgot not to relax. She took snapshots and traded teasing barbs both with Dillon and with the balloonist, and settled against Dillon as comfortably as if it were something she had been doing for years. It felt too right to alter, as if her body had been cut from his—the curves of one fitting into the hollows of the other.

Back on the ground, Zoey got out first and turned her camera on Dillon as he did likewise. She let the lens follow him as he approached a teenage couple pooling their resources to see if they had enough for a ride, and snapped pictures as he treated them to it.

"That was very nice of you," she said softly when he came back to her.

Dillon shrugged it away and joked, "Didn't seem fair to know how good it was to have you up there like that and then not let that poor kid try it."

They spent the rest of the morning walking the grounds while Dillon asked questions of the balloon owners and operators and Zoey took more candid shots of the people at work with late launches.

By noon all the balloons had descended and everything was wrapping up. Zoey and Dillon were heading for the gate when a boy of about four charged up to Dillon from behind and grabbed his jean-clad thigh. "You nearly lost me," the little boy said before looking all the way up to Dillon's face and realizing they didn't know each other.

In a split second Dillon had put the child at ease. "I'll bet your folks aren't too far away. Let's see if we can find them," he told the little boy. Then winking at Zoey he said, "Be right back."

She watched as he moved through the crowd, holding the child's hand. It was strange, but Zoey suddenly had the sense that what she saw in this man—the kindness, the thoughtfulness, the generosity, the conscientiousness, the caring—was actually what he was, in spite of the aspersions cast against him. And it wasn't only that she had fallen under the spell of his charm. Or that more than being attracted to him, she was beginning to care for him. She had seen those qualities with her own eyes; felt it in his touch and treatment of her. And if that was the recipe for unfit parenthood then there was something she didn't understand.

"Well, I think that crisis was averted," he told her when he had handed the little boy over to his mother and come back to Zoey.

He slipped his arm around her shoulders and headed for the gate again. This time when Zoey leaned into him, she did so with conscious thought. She liked this man. She felt good with him. How could that or anything else about him really be bad?

They had a champagne brunch at a hotel in downtown Denver and then, because his Sunday newspaper hadn't been delivered, Dillon persuaded Zoey to let him share hers. Not that it took much persuasion. She was no more inclined to be left alone on a long Sunday afternoon than he seemed to be to leave. In fact, Zoey suggested they go to the grocery store and buy the fixings for a cool seafood salad for dinner.

When they got back Dillon carried their two bags into Zoey's house and set them on the kitchen table amid the clutter of newspapers and camera equipment.

"How about a little wine with dinner?" he asked.

"Sorry, I'm fresh out."

He winked at her. "I'll be right back," he said as he headed out the back door and up the hill.

Zoey watched him as far as the terraced garden. Then she made a beeline for the bathroom. It had been a long day and she wanted to change her blue T-shirt for the fresh pink mock turtleneck. And she wanted to run a comb through her hair. And brush on a just a little blush. And put on just a little mascara, just a little lip gloss, just a little perfume.

Vanity thy name is Zoey, a voice in her head chided.

"Oh, be quiet. There's nothing wrong with freshening up," she said to her reflection just before going back to the kitchen to start dinner.

"You're boiling spaghetti?" Dillon asked when he came back a few minutes later, carrying a bottle of pale rosé.

"Pasta shells," she informed him officiously, noting that he, too, had made a pit stop. His hair lacked the windblown look the morning had put into it, his face no longer had even the shadow of a beard and he smelled heavenly. She tore her eyes away and worked to remember what they were talking about. Pasta shells. "Then we'll cool them and toss them in when the rest is ready."

"I see. What can I do?"

"Good question. What *can* you do in a kitchen, Mills?" she teased.

He made a squinty-eyed face at her. "Very funny. A couple of innocent P-B-and-Js and I'm condemned for life. This was suppose to be a joint venture, remember? What can I do to help?"

"You could open the wine."

"Do you think I can handle it?" He smiled slyly.

"I'm reserving judgment."

He uncorked the bottle with a flourish, handing her a full glass before taking one for himself.

Zoey toasted him. "Well done, Mills." Then she turned to take the boiling pasta from the stove.

He swatted her rear end with a dishcloth and made a growling noise deep in his throat. Then he leaned back against the counter. "Actually, I'll admit my cooking skills leave a little to be desired. I thought maybe we could use this as a lesson—Seafood Salad 101. Then I can add it to my limited repertoire and hope Jessy will eat it three times a week for the rest of her life."

He said it as if there was no question that he would be cooking for her that often in the future. It suddenly occurred to Zoey that maybe the reason he hadn't said anything about the custody suit wasn't because of shame or guilt but the fact that he wasn't worried about losing. Maybe everything, including her pictures, was just a formality. It seemed farfetched, but Dillon was nobody's fool. If there was cause for concern he'd have it. And if he had it, wouldn't it show? Somewhere?

"Will Jessy eat seafood salad?" she asked just to fill the silence she had let lapse.

"Probably not," Dillon answered with a laugh. "Unless you put a little jelly in it."

"Mmm. That's a variation I've never thought of." Zoey dried her hands on the legs of her black jeans and took another sip of her wine. "Okay, then. This is what you do...."

It was nearly dark by the time they were ready to eat. Zoey was feeling the effects of the wine and a long day. The thought of clearing the day's debris from the kitchen table so they could eat there was unappealing. So instead she headed for the living room and the coffee table with dishes, silverware and the salad. "This isn't sushi, but let's sit on the floor to eat anyway," she said.

Dillon followed with the wine and glasses. "Does that mean I can take my shoes off?"

"Great idea," she agreed, kicking her own to the side of the sofa. She felt so relaxed with him, as if they had known each other a lifetime.

He topped off both their glasses and joined her on the floor, their backs against the sofa.

"Did you grow up in Colorado?" she asked when they had both tried the salad and Dillon had judged it delicious.

He shook his head. "Minnesota. You?"

"Born and raised."

"And back again after a sojourn in Africa," he finished.

"When did you move here?"

"I went to Boulder for college, liked the fact that the snow never sticks around too long, married a native and stayed."

"Didn't you say your brother lives nearby?"

"With his wife and two daughters, aged ten and fourteen. They came for a visit, fell in love with Colorado and moved out here, too."

Zoey nodded. "Is he younger or older?"

"Younger by a year."

"How come his kids are so much older than Jessy?" What she was really wondering was why he had had Jessy so late.

"Linda had fertility problems. We didn't think we were ever going to be able to have kids. Jess was a surprise."

"But you wanted her?" Go away doubt.

He nodded vigorously. "There was never a baby more wanted than Jess. After giving up hope, she was like a gift. I don't think I'll ever stop feeling that way about her."

His voice was so full of sincerity that Zoey knew he meant it. She pushed her empty plate away and sank a little lower against the couch, taking her wine with her. A strand of her hair was on his shoulder and it seemed perfectly natural to pick it off. Just as natural as it seemed for him to turn slightly toward her and stretch his arm along the back of the cushions behind her head a moment later.

He had just refilled his glass and poured part of it in her nearly empty one. "You know, I had this really terrible thought last week when it looked like you were never home."

Even that reminder didn't matter to her in this new state of calm. "What was that?"

"I realized there was something pretty important that I hadn't asked you. Is there a man in your life?"

"You mean other than my father, brothers and brothers-in-law?"

"Yeah. I definitely meant other than men you're related to."

He sounded as relaxed as she felt. "No, there isn't."

Instant grin. Zoey couldn't help returning it. "How about you? How's your love life?" Not a good way to put it. She hid her embarrassment by taking another drink of wine. When she sneaked a peek at Dillon she found him enjoying her discomfort.

"Let's see," he said as if he were trying to sort it out. "If you mean my sex life, I'd have to say very sporadic. If you mean involvement with someone special, someone who makes me feel great and alive again, someone I've come to care about...that hasn't happened until now.''

A wave of tingling warmth swept through Zoey. She knew it came from his words and not the wine. The wine only allowed her to accept it. "Do I know her?" she flirted.

"Very well, I think." He put his glass on the table and moved her hair from her temple with a finger. "I just recently met her, but she hit me like a ton of bricks—you know, the way it happens when fate puts someone in your path and whispers in your ear that she's The One. She's kind of a strange lady, though. Furnished her house with a trampoline.''

Stop this, Zoey told herself. His tone was intimate. His face was only inches away from her own. The clean, masculine scent of his after-shave was all around her. But the fact of the matter was that she just plain didn't want to stop this. Or anything else.

It had been a long time since she had felt this content. This comfortable. This happy. Since she'd felt so close to a man who lit fire to everything inside of her. It had been much too long.

"A trampoline *inside* the house?" she heard herself say incredulously. "This sounds like someone too weird to believe. Maybe you should be careful."

He took her glass and set it beside his. "Oh, I don't know. When it's right, it's right," he said confidently, his voice low and deep and seductive.

Then he tipped her chin and looked into her eyes, holding them as surely as he held her chin. He lowered his mouth to hers. This time there was nothing tentative or questioning in the kiss. His lips were parted right from the start. But then so were Zoey's.

He cupped the back of her head in his palm, pressing her even more deeply into the kiss, while his other hand went to the side of her neck, down her shoulder and arm to her waist.

She wrapped one arm around him, and let the other rest

on his bicep. The taste of wine mingled with their breaths as his tongue found hers and coaxed it to play wet, warm, slippery games of chase.

She lost track of the rules when his hand pulled her T-shirt out of her jeans and found the soft flesh at her side. The feel of his fingers on her bare skin sent lightning bolts of desire all through her and made her writhe just slightly in response.

He left her mouth to kiss her nose, her cheek, her brow, her hair. "I want to make love to you, Zoey," he said in a raspy, passion-strained voice.

"I want you to," she answered as if the words had come from her senses rather than her brain, surprising her a little when she heard them. But it took only a second for her to realize that she meant it. She did want him to make love to her. She needed him to.

She took a deep breath as if to steady herself and looked him in the eye to let him know she had been serious. He kissed her once more and then stood, pulling her with him.

The only light came from the single table lamp beside the couch. It cast a faint glow into the bedroom. Dillon took her to the side of her brass four-poster and stopped. He held her face between his hands and lowered his mouth to hers again. This time he was demanding, thrusting his tongue in a way that no longer toyed with hers. And Zoey answered, suddenly aware of the beginnings of a craving deep inside that she hadn't felt in so long. Oh, how she wanted this man.

She pressed her hands into the broad, hard V of his back, pulling herself against his chest and bringing her breasts alive with yearning. He wrapped his arms around her then, drawing her more tightly to him for a moment before releasing her and dragging the hem of her T-shirt up a few inches.

Zoey felt the cooler air on her skin and suddenly broke free of his kiss, feeling unsure of herself. "I should tell you something," she whispered.

His tongue traced her jawline and dipped into the space just below her ear. "You can tell me anything."

"It's archaic." But her voice trailed away on a groan as he nudged the mock turtleneck of her T-shirt down and kissed the hollow of her throat. She swallowed. "I've... only done this with one other man...with Carl...."

His mouth came back to hers again, slowly, languidly, sweetly. "Thank you," he said between kisses.

"Thank you?" she breathed.

"For letting me be only the second."

She laughed just a little, feeling relieved and pleased that he felt that way. She shed the last of her inhibitions and reached for the buttons of his shirt.

Within moments both shirts were off, along with her bra. Dillon held her against him once more, raining kisses along her collarbone to her shoulders. The feel of his bare skin against hers brought her to a new and deeper level of desire, of passion, of need. Zoey answered it by pressing her lips to his chest and rubbing her chin against his hardened male nib.

He reached for the snap and zipper of her jeans. In short order he opened and slid them to her ankles where Zoey anxiously kicked them off.

Turnabout was fair play. She found the same fastenings on his jeans. But being tighter and strained with passion, the pants required his assistance to push down. He wore nothing underneath and she found it very arousing to realize he'd been that way all day.

That left only her panties. Black string bikinis.

He slipped his hands inside them, his palms cupped over her derriere. Then his thumbs traced the single string of elastic that circled her hips. Whatever he was thinking made him smile just before he stretched the elastic and let the last barrier drop to be kicked away with her jeans.

Zoey took a quick breath and felt his desire for her against her stomach. It was warm, hard, wonderful. And her heart was beating a mile a minute.

Dillon reached behind her, flung back the quilted coverlet and top sheet and eased her onto the bed. He lay partly on top of her, partly beside her. Then finally he covered her breast with that big, strong, powerful hand of his. Kneading, teasing, tormenting. Sometimes letting go to find the straining crest of her nipple. Sometimes gently pinching it. Sometimes rolling it between his finger and thumb. And when she thought she would die for wanting more, he lowered his lips there, tenderly nipping, tracing the darker circle with his tongue, then drawing her fully into his mouth until Zoey's back arched off the bed. An urgent need came to life in that spot between her thighs, compelling her to cross her leg over his and find a tiny respite.

Dillon gave a throaty, knowing chuckle. He reached a hand to her derriere and pressed while pushing that muscular thigh more firmly against her, giving what she had been too modest to take for herself.

But the greater passion it evoked gave Zoey a dose of courage. She pressed herself up into those same parts of his. This time the sound that came from his throat was a groan that told her his need was no less than her own.

Then his hand found the core of her. For a moment what erupted inside of Zoey was so strong she couldn't breathe. Her head fell back, her mouth opened.

Dillon kissed her neck, the underside of her chin, her slack bottom lip. Then his tongue traced the sensitive inside of her upper lip.

"Now?" he asked on a bare breath.

"Oh, yes," she whispered so softly it was nearly inaudible.

Gently he pressed her back against the mattress and came over her, spreading her thighs, his legs between hers, his arms on either side of her head. He lowered his hips to hers, kissed her, open-mouthed, thrusting his tongue.

Zoey arched upward, inviting. She felt him flex against her, felt the tightening of his muscles, and opened her thighs wider still.

"Now," she breathed, as a part demand, part reminder, part request.

Finally, slowly, he came into her until his hips were cradled in hers. The feel of him fully inside of her was so wonderful.

"Did I hurt you?" he was quick to ask.

"No, no," she barely managed to reply, arching again to let him know what she felt was only good. Only something she wanted more of.

He sighed and lowered his upper body to hers, thrusting even deeper inside her. Again and again, he pulsed there, first in measured and slow movements, then he gained speed until his pace was too rapid for Zoey to match and all she could do was ride the waves of climax that swept like a tempest through her. And when the storm was spent she found him just reaching his own, all tensile strength and taut, sinewy muscle, delving so deeply into her she felt as if they really had become one.

He exhaled as if deflating, and relaxed a single muscle at a time. He smoothed her hair lethargically, and then he raised up on his forearms and kissed her. But it wasn't like any kiss she had ever had before. It seemed to be a statement of his thoughts and emotions, and it made her feel loved and cherished. It made her feel closer to him, bound to him in more than just the physical sense. And it brought hot moisture to her eyes.

He ended the kiss with several shorter ones and then looked at her. "Are you okay?" he asked as if he really wanted to know.

Zoey didn't trust her voice, so she only nodded her head. This was all new to her. Something she had never found even with Carl.

But Dillon must not have been convinced because he frowned and said, "Are you sure?"

She blinked the moisture out of her eyes, swallowed some of the wealth of emotion she felt and nodded again.

"Yes," she managed to reply in a small voice. "It was just...powerful."

His frown relaxed into a knowing smile. "Powerful is the word," he agreed.

He withdrew then but didn't let go of her as he rolled onto his back. Instead he pulled her toward him until she was curved against him in a perfect meeting of their bodies. He reached for the sheet, covering them both and then settled down so she could rest her head on his chest.

Zoey listened to the beat of his heart while he stroked her hair, massaged her shoulder, tightened his arms around her every so often.

"What do you see in your future, Zoey?" he asked after a while, his voice still love-ragged and husky.

She smiled. "At the moment I don't think I could find the energy to run out of here if the place caught on fire," she said.

It was good to hear him laugh at that. "I meant after some sleep."

"As in tomorrow?"

"As in all your tomorrows."

She sighed and reluctantly resigned herself to coming back down to earth. "My first priority is rebuilding my business."

"I know, you've told me that a couple of times. What about personally?"

Zoey rubbed her cheek against the hair on his chest. "This is nice," she hedged. "What about you? What do you see for yourself?"

"My job is fine. I'm concentrating on getting my life back on track."

"Has it been off track?"

"Way off."

There was a moment's silence then. Zoey knew he was going to tell her about the custody case, but she felt no tension, no fearful anticipation. Somehow it seemed right that now, with her lying in his arms after making love, he should confide in her.

"There are some things I haven't told you," he began. "The accident that killed Linda two years ago..." He took a deep breath before going on. "I was driving the car."

She went very still. Of all the things she'd thought, that hadn't occurred to her. After a moment she tipped her head back and looked up at him. "Was the accident your fault?" she asked, very softly, very carefully.

He shook his head. "No, thank God. I don't know if I could have lived with that. A drunk driver ran a red light and hit us broadside. She was killed instantly."

Something else occurred to Zoey. "And you?"

"I was in pretty bad shape. Both legs were broken, several ribs, and this arm," he tightened the one that was around her. "Two discs were crushed in my spine and my skull was fractured."

"My God."

"It took three surgeries to piece me back together," he said matter-of-factly, as if relating someone else's experiences. His voice was devoid of all self-pity.

"The scar on your back," she said to herself.

"That was one of the surgeries, yes. There's another scar where they put pins in my left leg and a third hidden in my hair where pressure had to be released from around my brain. I didn't look too great as a bald man, let me tell you," he finished, lightening the tone with a chuckle.

"How long were you in the hospital?"

"Not quite a year."

No wonder he hadn't heard or read about Carl's death.

He tucked his chin against his chest and looked down at her. "I'm not telling you all this for sympathy. It really is going somewhere." He rested his head back and went on. "During the first two months right after the accident I was in and out of consciousness—mostly out. It was touch and go. My doctors weren't too sure I was going to make it and there was certainly no way I was capable of coming to a decision on Jessy's behalf if the need arose—if she were hurt and needed permission for medical treatment, or something like that. The courts granted my in-laws temporary guardianship of Jess, and they were right to do it.''

A knot of tension clenched Zoey's stomach. That wasn't what Harold Miflin had told her. The investigator had said Jessy had been taken away from Dillon. But he was still talking and she knew she had to pay close attention.

''Even when I left the hospital I was a wreck,'' he went on. ''Not much better than an invalid. I had to move in with my brother and his wife. Frank, Sharon and their kids played nurse for as long as I needed it. There was no way I could have taken Jessy back then.''

''Of course not,'' Zoey agreed.

''Anyway, it took three more months, but I worked my tail off, first in rehabilitation and then in a training program to rebuild my strength.''

And he'd done an admirable job. Zoey couldn't believe that he had been any better before.

''The trouble is,'' he continued, ''when I was back on my feet and ready, my in-laws didn't want to give Jessy up. Instead they petitioned the court for permanent custody.''

His admission dropped like a rock. Or was that just her imagination? ''On what grounds?'' Zoey asked.

''That I'm an unfit father,'' he answered ruefully but without hesitation. ''How else could my daughter be taken away from me?''

''Unfit in what way?''

He shrugged. ''That part I don't know exactly. They haven't spoken to me since they started this whole thing and all the papers say is that they have reason to believe me unfit. Everything's gone through lawyers and courts, and I don't know what they're basing it on. What I do know is that when their attorney approached mine about my relinquishing custody, they were arguing that with them Jess would have a two-parent home and a more stable environment than she would have with a father who travels for business.''

He paused a moment. "I don't condemn them. They lost their only child and I'm sure Jess has filled the gap for them. They've raised her for the past two years, they love her, and since they're a different generation, they honestly don't believe a man alone can raise a daughter properly. I'm sure they think they're doing what's best for Jessy.''

How could he be so calm about it? "You aren't worried?" Zoey couldn't help asking.

"I'm not taking it lightly, by any means. I just know they don't have a leg to stand on.''

"But if it's in court...''

"False allegations are made all the time—or so my brother, the barracuda lawyer, tells me. Both sides have to be heard. And in the case of a child's welfare—well, as much as I hate that it's happening to Jessy and me and has kept us apart for so long on top of my recovery time, any doubt that something bad is happening to a child should be explored.''

Zoey didn't say anything because she didn't know what to say. It all seemed so clear-cut. She wanted to believe him, and what he'd said lent weight to her theory that the investigation, her being hired to take pictures, was all just a formality. But wasn't hiring a professional photographer a bit much for nothing more than a formality? And why were there discrepancies between this story and the one Miflin had told her?

"Zoey?" Dillon said when the silence had gone on and on.

"This all must have been very hard for you," she murmured, trying to leash her thoughts.

He didn't admit to that. Instead he said, "Hopefully it'll be over soon. We had a court date for this Wednesday but the other side managed to postpone it until next week. Waiting is the worst.''

Zoey swallowed with difficulty. Did her pictures have anything to do with the postponement?

He looked at her face. Zoey couldn't help raising her eyes to his, finding what seemed like confusion creasing his brows. "Maybe this wasn't a good time to tell you."

He didn't understand her response, she knew. But then how could he? "No, I'm glad you confided in me," she said, trying to infuse her voice with something that resembled reassurance. "It's just come as a shock."

He nodded, kissed her and settled back, obviously accepting her excuse. "I didn't mean for you to worry about it. But I wanted you to know."

His tone went from sounding confidential back to matter-of-fact. "I came out of the accident with nearly thirty thousand dollars in medical bills after what the insurance paid. I had to take the Orlando job to pay those off and get them out of the way. Now that they are, I can go back to a more human schedule and hire some help so I won't have to do all the traveling. That should refute any claim that I'm not around enough to raise her. And these days half the kids in the country are growing up in single-parent households, so that shouldn't hold water, either."

Zoey swallowed hard. Did he really believe that was all there was to it? Or was that just all he was telling her? "So you and your brother feel that you have a strong case."

"The burden is on them to prove I'm unfit."

Or negligent. And some of her pictures might do just that. Zoey's heart was pounding again, but this time passion had nothing to do with it.

Her tension didn't seem to communicate itself to Dillon. "I just wanted you to know what was going on," he repeated. Then he yawned and settled deeper into the mattress. "I don't know about you, but getting up at four this morning is catching up with me."

"Mmm," she agreed even though sleep was the furthest thing from her mind.

"I hope you didn't want me to leave...."

"No," she reassured in a hurry, realizing in that instant just how torn she was. Even in the shadow of doubt she still wanted to be here in his arms.

Those arms tightened around her then. "Good, because I don't want to go. This feels so right."

It did to Zoey, too. Heaven help her.

As if on cue the lamp in the living room automatically turned off and left them in darkness. Dillon laughed and murmured, "Perfect." Then he raised his head from the pillow and turned her face up to his. "Good night, Zoey," he said in the intimate tone of voice she'd come to know well.

"Good night," she whispered back.

His breath was a warm feather brush against her skin as he kissed her. Then he settled back, still holding her. Within minutes Zoey felt the steady rise and fall of his chest and heard the even breaths that told her he was sleeping. But as tired as she was after a full day and an even fuller evening with Dillon, rest wasn't something she could do. Not when she kept remembering that Harold Miflin had said Jessy had been *taken away* from Dillon.

Why were the two stories different? Dillon's seemed much too elaborate to be a lie. But he was the only one who had any reason to resort to deceit. And if he was telling the truth, why wouldn't the court simply have given him Jessy back when he regained his health?

But why would Miflin have lied? Was it possible that Dillon didn't know just how serious this matter really was? Or know the extent of the allegations against him and the investigation that was going on to substantiate them?

Zoey didn't have any answers. The only person who could have would be the investigator himself. And she had every intention of asking him the questions. Because whether Dillon knew or not, he was out on a limb.

And Zoey's heart was out there with him.

Chapter Seven

"Ms. Carmichael? This is Harold Miflin...."

The machine had answered the phone before Zoey was awake enough to think about anything but the fact that there was a man in her bed. The minute she heard the investigator's name she lunged and knocked the receiver to the floor under the bed. She had to reel it in by the cord.

"Hello. I'm here," she said when she got it to her ear. She was instantly wide-awake, alert and full of adrenaline.

"I expected a call from you by now. Didn't you get my messages?" he asked curtly.

Messages—plural? She had heard the one from Saturday. But she'd been so preoccupied with Dillon on Sunday that she hadn't even checked the machine. "I'm sorry. I've been very busy," she answered him.

"I need those pictures. I'll be there in half an hour to pick them up."

"No!" Zoey cleared her throat and forced a businesslike

tone into her voice to hide her panic. "I'm afraid it can't be done that way today. I'll come to you."

"Is there a problem with the pictures?"

"No, it's not that." Think fast. "I was just on my way out. In fact I'm late already. So if you'll tell me where your office is, I'll bring them there."

Miflin let silence lapse and Zoey was afraid he could tell she was lying. But finally he sighed and said peevishly, "All right. I'm in the old house that's been converted to an office building on the northwest corner of 44th between Wadsworth and Kipling."

"That's easy enough. I'll see you later this morning."

"With the pictures," he reminded tersely.

"Of course. Goodbye." Zoey hung up and fell back on the pillow, realizing only then that she held the sheet over her bare breasts in a tightly clenched fist.

"Business," Dillon guessed in a raspy voice from beside her, his eyes still closed.

"Business," she confirmed.

He rolled from his stomach to his side and propped his head up on a hand. Then he looked at her through one eye and smiled sleepily. "And you were almost caught in the act, so you lied to keep whoever it was from coming over."

"Right." She hoped he never knew how right.

"I hope you bought us a little time." He opened his other eye finally and dropped a kiss on her bare shoulder.

"Not really," Zoey answered, trying not to think about how good that kiss felt, or how nice it was to wake up with him there, or how unreasonably appealing he looked with his hair tousled and his expression lazy, relaxed and contented.

"Wrong answer," he informed her. "I'm not finished with you."

She couldn't resist running her palm over his shoulder and down his bicep. "You'll have to be," she said without much conviction.

Shaking his head, he pulled her until her side was against

his chest. He rested his arm across her stomach, nuzzled her cheek with his nose and then looked down at her. "How are you this morning?"

She smiled at him and his consideration. "I'm just fine. How are you?"

"Never better."

"So. What exactly is the protocol for getting up with someone you're not married to?"

He grinned. "You mean not only was Carl your first lover, but you were married to him before he even got to be that?"

There was nothing but delight in his tone, so she didn't take offense at his teasing. "In a family with eleven kids you can bet I grew up very aware of how easy it was to get pregnant. I wasn't taking *any* chances."

"Until last night. Or am I mistaken?"

He wasn't. And it was just another indication of how potent his effect on her was. Not once had she gotten that carried away with Carl. She grimaced. "I've never been that irresponsible in my life."

"That makes two of us," he said, but without the remorse. "Maybe I should tell you what I was leading up to last night."

"Last night was only a lead-up?" she managed to reply, because in spite of everything she couldn't regret what they'd done.

"The conversation that started after was the segue, believe it or not. I wanted you to know my deepest secrets before I got around to the main course. But somehow the timing seemed off when the secrets were all out."

That was her fault, Zoey knew. Her reaction to what he'd told her hadn't been something that invited him to say more. "So we're going to have the main course for breakfast?"

"Think you can handle it?"

"I won't know until I hear it."

"Okay. Fair enough." He kissed her lightly. "I asked

about what you saw in your future because I want a place in it. Unless these feelings don't mean the same thing they did eighteen years ago, I'm falling in love with you."

Zoey's heart leapt for joy. And then she thought better of it. This didn't make an already complicated situation any easier.

"What am I going to do with you?" She tried to force her voice to sound lighter than she felt. "You can't tell a person something like that when they have to rush off to a business meeting."

"Too late. I just did." He kissed her again. "You don't have to say anything, Zoey. I know it comes as a surprise and I know I'm rushing things. But I feel good about us and I wanted to tell you."

"It is...powerful between us, isn't it?" she said, repeating last night's adjective for lack of a better word and the courage to admit that she was afraid she was falling in love with him, too.

"In more than just sex," he agreed.

"It scares me."

"I know it does." He kissed her once more, this time in a lingering, warm and sweet way. When he ended it he winked at her. "Not get up and run for the bathroom before you get further behind for this meeting. I'll close my eyes while you do and when you come out I'll be up the hill. Then I'll call you later and we can have dinner tonight."

Maybe the falling part was already past and she was smack-dab in love with this man. Zoey kissed him. "Thank you. You're a nice guy, do you know that, Mills?"

"Damn. Now if I want to live up to that, I can't peek like I planned."

"Definitely no peeking," she confirmed. "Now close your eyes."

He did, falling theatrically back on the pillow and clamping both hands over his eyes, too. "Enough?"

"Enough," she said as she slipped out of bed and ran for the bathroom.

* * *

The investigator's words on the day he hired her echoed in Zoey's mind as she opened the door to Miflin's Investigative Services an hour later. She remembered him mentioning a supervisor, and yet the tiny office was obviously a one-man operation—Miflin's operation.

"Good, you're prompt," he greeted her from behind the scarred desk that took up one corner of the faded yellow office.

Zoey muttered something about trying to be, as she glanced around. There was no secretary, or even a typewriter. Three gray-metal filing cabinets lined a wall and a card table supported a coffeepot, cups and packets of sugar and powdered cream. Miflin didn't stand up, nor did he offer her one of the mismatched chairs that faced his desk.

"Who exactly are we working for, Mr. Miflin?" she blurted out in response to a bad feeling she suddenly had about this man.

"You're working for me."

"And who are you working for?"

He shrugged. "You'll find out when you see your check, so I don't suppose it matters—Mills's in-laws, the Whites."

"The Whites," she repeated in an effort to see if she could control her voice and keep from being hostile. "You said the court wanted to hire me."

He smiled slightly. "No. *You* said that. I never claimed to be investigating for the court."

"You specifically mentioned a supervisor and being *assigned* this job."

"The Whites could be considered supervisors, and hiring me is the same as assigning me the job."

"And you didn't deny working for the court when I assumed it."

He just kept on smiling, and Zoey wondered how she had ever gotten the impression he was a kindly gentleman.

"So you purposely misled me."

He shrugged again. "My assistant quit on me the week before last. I had three cases to juggle and no way to keep

Mills under surveillance at the same time. Your sign went up and it was like an omen, handing me the idea of hiring you." His small eyes bored into her. "I just needed you to take the pictures, lady. That's all. It didn't matter to me what you thought. Now, where are they?"

Always follow your instincts—her mother's words from as far back as Zoey could remember. She had never appreciated the advice more than at that moment. "I didn't bring them," she said honestly. "I had some questions to ask you first. I'm not altogether sure Dillon Mills is the villain you paint him to be."

"Did I paint him a villain?" he mocked.

"This time I didn't just assume it. You specifically told me that the little girl had been *taken away* from her father."

"He doesn't have custody of her."

"But not because she was *taken away* from him."

"How'd you find that out?"

"I just did."

"Neighborhood gossip," Miflin surmised as he rummaged through a pile on the corner of his desk until he found a file. "I hate using outsiders. Sooner or later something always interferes. The minute I saw you were a woman, I knew that guy's good looks were going to get me into trouble," he muttered sarcastically as he opened the file. "Didn't anyone ever tell you not to judge a book by its cover? Sit down, Ms. Carmichael."

"I want to know the truth about what's going on," she demanded as she took one of the chairs.

"You want some truths? I'll give you some. My clients have guardianship of Jessica Mills. They have had for the past two years—"

Zoey cut him off. "Which was granted them because her father was so badly injured in the same accident that killed her mother that he couldn't care for her. *Not* because she was *taken away* from him."

"Take it easy, Mama Bear. Mills is a big boy, he doesn't need you to defend him. His daughter now, that's a different story. That poor kid needs some intervention." He held up most of the papers in the file. "See these? Know what they are? Reports. Official reports."

Zoey watched as he set them back down, scanned them and seemed to paraphrase what he read.

"In the past year Dillon Mills has been gone a total of two hundred and thirty-eight days. Even when he was in Denver, he spent twelve and fourteen hours at a time at his office and made almost no attempt to see his daughter, not even on weekends. Not much of a father." Miflin shuffled papers. "On the rare occasions when he spent minimal time alone with her, she was returned to her grandparents displaying obvious signs that no care whatsoever had been given to her hygiene." Miflin looked up through bushy eyebrows at Zoey. "I have witnesses."

She didn't say anything.

He officiously turned that paper face-down on the desk and went on to the next. "A doctor's examinations made upon her return from visits with her father report that Jessica showed marked signs of negligence and the existence of recent bruises of unknown origin." There was strong insinuation in his tone that condemned Dillon as the cause of those bruises.

Miflin went on to another page. "Questioning of the child herself repeatedly brings the answer that 'Dad's mean to me.'" More paper shuffling.

"Furthermore, Jessica has been under the care of a child psychologist for treatment of nightmares about her father. It's the therapist's conclusion that being with Mills causes fear and insecurity in the child. It's been found to be detrimental to her mental health, well-being and development, and that she would be better off without any contact with him."

As if it were a grand finale, Miflin slid another paper across his desk for Zoey to inspect. "And this is a police report filed a week ago, Saturday, when the child was missing from home due to a lack of adequate supervision. This you must know something about yourself, since you're listed as the neighbor who brought her home.

"What I'm sure you don't know is that before this visit Mills agreed that he would not be working during the time he had Jessica, nor would he leave her in the care of a baby-sitter, let alone one who loses her. He was in violation of the agreement less than twelve hours after picking her up from her grandparents. It also seems pretty clear that work came before his daughter *and* this custody suit against him." Miflin arched a brow and finished disparagingly, "Is this a situation you want to protect, Ms. Carmichael?"

Doctor's reports and conclusions from a psychologist?

But before she could sort her thoughts, Miflin went on. "I don't know who you've been talking to about this or what you've been told, but doctors, police and psychologists don't lie."

"And you didn't need me to stack the deck against him because it was already stacked," Zoey struck out. "What I don't understand is why you needed pictures, at all."

"I'd have taken them myself, if my assistant had stuck around. I wanted illustrations to lend impact to the reports," he explained. "And I'll bet that's what you've done, and that's why you felt the need to protect him by not bringing the pictures with you."

"And why are you so ready to read me all the evidence against him today, when you said you couldn't tell me anything at all the day you hired me?" Zoey shot back.

He shrugged once more. "I honestly didn't want biased pictures. If I had told you all this you might only have taken ones that showed it. If the guy isn't guilty, I didn't want it to look that way."

"But you don't have any compunction about it now."

"If you had brought the pictures I would have kept my mouth shut. But I could see the minute you walked in here that you were wondering how a good-looking guy who lives in a big, fancy house and probably fell all over himself thanking you for bringing the kid back, could really be a rotten father. But let me assure you, Ms. Carmichael, child abuse happens even in nice houses owned by outwardly nice people. The guy can't handle the job of parent, no matter how he looks. Period.''

"I don't believe he's a child abuser," she said tightly.

"Call it anything you like. Just get those pictures to me."

"And if I don't?" she asked with more conviction than she felt.

"I'll give you until tomorrow morning. If they aren't here by eight o'clock, I'll have the Whites' lawyer subpoena them. Refuse that, Ms. Carmichael, and you're in contempt of court. That means fines, penalties and a vacation in jail."

Jane's front door was open when Zoey got there an hour later. "It's me. Anybody home?" she called through the screen.

"Great minds work alike," Jane said as she let her in. "I left a message on your machine not ten minutes ago."

"I wasn't home," Zoey answered distractedly. For a moment she paused in her sister's living room, wondering why it seemed empty. The couch and chairs were still in place, along with the end tables and floor lamps. "Where's the coffee table?" she asked when she finally realized that piece was missing.

Jane ran a hand through her short, pale brown hair. "Exiled to the basement until Tim is eighteen," she said. "Come into the kitchen while I clean up his lunch stuff. Have you eaten?"

"I'm not hungry." Zoey followed her sister into a pink kitchen and sat at the table across from the chicken-noodle soup mess obviously left by her nephew. "Is Tim down for his nap already?"

"Yep." Jane went to work on the debris. "Sorry about Saturday night."

Zoey had forgotten. "Where were you?" she asked without much vigor.

"At the hospital emergency room having six stitches put in Timmy's head."

"What happened?"

"He was in a wild mood and I came in here to answer the phone. I couldn't have been gone thirty seconds before I heard a big crash. He had jumped from the couch and hit his head on the edge of the coffee table."

"Is he okay?"

"He is now. He just has a gash up near his hairline."

"Poor kid."

"Anyway, I'm sorry about not leaving a note or anything. We rushed out of here so fast I didn't even put my shoes on. I felt like a total idiot sitting at the hospital in my bare feet." With the lunch mess cleaned, Jane went to the refrigerator. "Iced tea?"

"Sure."

"So how are things on the spy front?" her sister asked as she brought two glasses to the table and sat down.

"Not good," Zoey said. She stared at her tea a moment and then brought Jane up to date on everything to do with Dillon, including the meeting with Harold Miflin.

"This neighbor of yours sounds like a real creep," her sister said when Zoey was finished.

"That's just it, he isn't a creep at all," she defended without having to think twice.

"Are you sure?" Jane asked dubiously.

This time Zoey did think about it. "I was really beginning to believe he was being wrongly accused."

"And now?"

"Doctor reports and psychological evaluations stretch a pretty deep, dark shadow of doubt," she admitted.

"I tend to believe that reports from doctors and psychologists are indisputable."

"But he loves that little girl. He really does."

"Do you think child abusers go around bragging about

it, Zoey? I'll bet most of them act like they're crazy about
their kids to other people.''

"He isn't an abuser. If anything he might be negligent…'' Her voice trailed off as Zoey caught sight of some
of the childproofing Jane had done in her own house. There
was a guard along the front of the stove so Tim couldn't
reach the burners. There were safety catches on all the cupboard doors, and plugs in all the electrical outlets. She already knew how medicines were locked in a box and set
on the top shelf of the linen closet. The sharp edges of the
brick hearth were padded. The basement door was latched
so high up Zoey had had to stand on tiptoe to reach it
herself. Even the throw rugs Jane loved had been taken up
to keep Tim from tripping over them. There wasn't any of
that in Dillon's house. And there wasn't any sign that he
intended to do any of it.

"Negligence is still abuse,'' Jane was saying.

"But isn't there a difference between overt negligence
like leaving a kid home alone for two days and oversight
negligence?''

"Sure. Having that coffee table around was oversight
negligence. It just didn't occur to me that a small oval
coffee table could be dangerous. But Zoey, that's a one-
time thing. You're talking about the oversights going on
and on, and happening with enough severity to convince
professionals the child is better off with her grandparents.
That may not be as overt as leaving a kid alone for two
days, but it's negligence.''

Still, Zoey's every inclination was to defend Dillon. It
didn't matter that her sister was only voicing what she had
thought herself. She didn't want to believe it and she certainly didn't want to listen to her own doubts confirmed.
"Oh, my gosh, look at the time,'' she said all of a sudden.
"I didn't realize it was so late. I have to get across town
with my portfolio for an interview with the head of advertising at Mayco's department store. They're switching from
illustrations to photographs for all their ads, and I have a

shot at jewelry and housewares." It was all true, except that the meeting was three hours away. She stood and poured her untouched tea down the drain. "I don't want to be late."

"Zoey?" Jane said as she trailed her to the front door. "I know you feel something for this guy."

An understatement. She felt *everything* for Dillon. Buckets and buckets of everything.

Jane was still talking. "But don't make them subpoena those pictures. Turn them over and let the court decide. If he's innocent, he'll get his daughter back. If he isn't…well, then go from there. But whatever you do, don't jeopardize yourself for his sake."

"Of course I wouldn't do that—"

"Of course you would," Jane cut her off.

"I have to go," Zoey said as she rushed out the door.

"Call me and let me know what happens," Jane said after her.

"Oh, I will, I will," Zoey answered halfheartedly as she nearly dove into her car.

It was six that evening before Zoey got back home. The meeting at Mayco had lasted longer than she'd expected, but the results had been good. Better than good, actually. The minute she had shown some of her early work—photographs of crystal for Mayco's competitor—she'd sewn up the jewelry and housewares accounts. And she'd been given another interview on Wednesday morning for the much bigger women's clothes and shoes ads. If she got that, too, not only would she have a steady income, but reentrance into the photography business in a big way.

"Lucky my work speaks for itself, because my winning personality made itself scarce today," she mumbled as she put away her portfolio. With Harold Miflin's threats and Dillon and his situation on her mind, her interview had not been her best.

But even getting the job and a chance at others didn't

help her mood. Zoey was down in the dumps, confused and at odds with herself. "That's what you get for hiding out in a dollar movie until the meeting so you wouldn't have to think about anything or make any decisions about what to do with those pictures or whether or not to tell Dillon what's going on," she told her reflection in the side of the toaster.

Then her phone rang and saved her from thinking about it again.

"Hello, Zowy?" she heard a sweet little voice say when she answered it.

Dillon's followed immediately. "Jess, get off that phone. I told you you could talk *after* I do."

"No way. I wanna talk to Zowy now."

"Hi, Jessy," Zoey said, unable to suppress a wan smile at the gleeful sound of the child's voice.

"Got some docker's things."

"Docker's things?"

"She means doctor's things," Dillon translated. "Okay, now you told her, Jess. Get off."

"My toorn," Jessy insisted.

"It's not your turn. It's mine. Now get off."

"I wanna come over yur house an' jup, Zowy."

"Hold on a minute, will you, Zoey?" Dillon said, exasperated. "I'll hang up in here and go wrestle the extension from her."

"Woops. Bye, bye, Zowy," the little girl said in a hurry.

The sounds of Dillon entering whatever room it was that Jessy was in came next. "Watch it. Throwin' big toy," the little girl warned just before Zoey heard a metallic clunk. After a few minutes Dillon came back on the line.

"Okay. She's sticking bandages on my leg, I can talk."

Zoey couldn't contain her own suspicions. "Where did she get doctor's things? Has she been sick?"

"I bought her a toy medical kit."

Relief. "What's Jessy doing there, anyway? You didn't say anything about having her today."

"It was an impromptu visit. I got a call from Frank, who got a call from the Whites' attorney, who asked if I wanted Jess for the night. No explanation. All I care about is getting to see her, so I said yes. But..." He sighed. "I think I better cancel our dinner date. For some reason I keep having the weirdest feeling that something just isn't right, and until this custody garbage is settled I don't want to rock the boat."

Zoey's stomach clenched at the thought that his instincts were warning him about her. "Sure. No problem." It was probably better if she didn't see him, anyway. She had some decisions to make and the emotions he stirred wouldn't help anything.

"I'm sorry," he went on, sounding genuinely contrite. "After barely saying hello this morning, I was counting on a quiet evening together."

Something shattered in the background, which gave Zoey an out. "I don't think you're in for that," she said. "What happened?"

"Jessy knocked a lamp off the table."

"There must be glass all over."

"There is."

"Don't let her get into it," Zoey felt compelled to say when he didn't seem in any hurry to hang up and take care of it.

"She's on to new adventures. Can I call you later? After she goes to bed?"

Guilt made this conversation hard on Zoey. She didn't want to have another one. At least not until she decided what she was going to do. "Sure, if my lights are on," she said, thinking fast. "But I may go to bed early myself."

"Damn, and I'll have to miss it," he joked.

"You can go to bed early, too." Zoey couldn't resist teasing him back. "I'll bet you're all worn out."

"How old do you think I am?" he feigned indignation. "I have enough stamina for more than one night. I can stay up late for two in a row, sometimes."

"Glad to hear it." Actually she wasn't glad to hear anything from him. The sound of his voice made her want to see him and forget all about this predicament she'd gotten herself into. "I better let you go clean up that glass before Jessy decides to see what she can make out of it."

"True." But he didn't hang up. Instead, after a moment he said, "I meant what I said this morning, Zoey. My feelings for you are strong, and getting stronger by the minute."

Another loud noise followed by a loud wail from Jessy saved her from having to comment on that.

"I better go. If I don't talk to you tonight I'll call tomorrow. Unless you're busy, let's have dinner then."

Zoey listened to the dial tone for a moment before putting the receiver back in the cradle. She had the feeling that breaking that contact with him was more of an ending than it seemed. And it clenched like a fist around her heart.

How could she feel this way about a man who abused his child? she asked herself.

But she knew the answer. In spite of all she'd heard about him today, in spite of what she'd seen for herself, in spite of Jane and Miflin both thinking he was an unfit father, there was still a part of her that didn't believe it. With a resigned sigh, she admitted the time had come to face what she'd been pushing away all day.

She headed for her filing cabinet and the folder that held all the pictures and negatives she had taken of Dillon and Jessy. While she dug through the papers that hid it, Jane's words repeated themselves in her mind. Reports from doctors and psychologists were indisputable, her sister had said.

Indisputable.

Obvious signs that no care whatsoever had been given to her hygiene. Marked signs of negligence.

What exactly did all that mean? Was poor hygiene a dirty face and ice cream dribbled down her shirt front? Or did it mean diapers left unchanged for so long she had rashes?

And what were marked signs of negligence? Had she shown extreme weight loss? Dehydration? Or was her hair sometimes uncombed?

Zoey had seen nothing of the more drastic possibilities. And she had been watching closely and constantly. If she hadn't spied anything worse, how could anyone else have? And though she had witnessed the less drastic end of the spectrum, well, all kids got dirty and were sometimes unkempt.

And what about the psychologist's conclusions? Was Dillon giving his daughter nightmares? Zoey couldn't dispute that the child had them; her surveillance hadn't lasted through the nights. But it was hard to believe that the cause—if the child did have them—was her father. After all, Zoey had observed Jessy's affection for Dillon. And if being with him was so bad, why had the little girl clung to his neck when he was leaving her with the people who were supposedly better for her?

One by one Zoey set the pictures out on the kitchen table. Maybe she didn't have the expertise to scoff at official reports, but the idea that Jessy's visits with her father were nightmarish just didn't fly.

And as for Miflin insinuating that Dillon was the cause of Jessy's bruises, Zoey knew for a fact that that wasn't the case. She had noted the little girl fall and bang into enough things on her own to know that was a more likely origin. Besides, when she'd been with the two of them or behind her viewfinder, Dillon had shown Jessy only patience and gentleness, no matter how irascible and stubborn the child was. Saying Dillon was a child abuser was as ridiculous as saying the overprotective Jane was a child abuser because Tim had cut his head on the coffee table.

"But..." Zoey sighed as she looked over the pictures she had taken in the past week. She had to admit that there were other parts of the reports that she couldn't dispute, because right there in front of her own two eyes was evidence.

Yes, some of the shots showed Dillon as a great dad. But some of them didn't. Those where Jessy was in precarious positions, on the verge of causing herself harm when Dillon was nowhere in sight, bore witness to neglect by oversight. And maybe Jane was right—neglect by oversight was still neglect.

Zoey picked up a picture of Jessy standing nose to nose with Arachnid. The dog, appearing to be the aggressor, was leaning forward. Jessy was leaning back as if in fright. Arachnid looked so menacing, as if he was about to take a bite out of the sweet little girl.

The picture had been the last on a roll of film, and before Zoey had finished reloading, she'd seen Arachnid lick Jessy's face and do nothing more.

Appeared and *looked like*. Those were the operative words here. Even if she hadn't witnessed the dog following through by licking Jessy's face, she would have known from her own experience with him that nothing bad was about to happen. Arachnid was one of the meekest, mildest, gentlest dogs she'd ever been around. In spite of his breed's reputation as dangerous attack dogs, Arachnid was really a pussycat. If anything, it was the poor animal that was menaced by Jessy's two-and-a-half-year-old willfulness.

But no one could tell that from the picture.

"So sometimes, even when the photographer is trying to shoot the truth, pictures can be deceiving," she said defensively.

And that was a good point.

What if someone had been taking secret snapshots of Tim when Jane had gone to answer the phone and the little boy had fallen against the table? Wouldn't those have illustrated the same kind of neglect that these of Jessy supposedly did? And if the hospital report of Tim's injury was taken at face value and in conjunction with the shadow of doubt cast by people who had their own reasons to suggest Jane was an unfit mother, wasn't it possible that even her conscientious sister would look bad? In fact, what if every fall or precarious situation any kid got into was watched from the outside under the shadow of doubt? Wouldn't most parents look negligent?

"Probably," Zoey answered herself. Because no parent—father or mother—could be with a child every minute. The best that could be done was to make the home as safe as possible, so that in those moments when the children couldn't be watched with an eagle eye they also couldn't do themselves serious damage.

But Dillon hadn't made his home as safe as possible.

"But he could," she said as if there was someone in the room with her. "He just needs some things brought to his attention and some guidance about what safeguards should be taken."

Oh, how she hoped that was true. Because if she were Jessy, Zoey realized, she would want to stay with him. What she wouldn't have given for a dad like Dillon. One who paid attention to her. Who took her to the zoo. Who read to her. Who played in the sandbox with her.

Thinking from that point of view put a new light on it. And when all the aspersions were taken out and she looked at what she knew for a fact, she believed that Dillon was not an unfit father. An inexperienced one, yes. An indulgent one, certainly. But not a maliciously, or even a hopelessly negligent one. Should Jessy be denied a father who genuinely loved her, who gladly spent time with her and who honestly took an interest in her, because his house didn't have childproof locks, cupboard latches or general kiddie safeguards that could so easily be added?

No way, as Jessy would say.

Dillon might need a fast course in diligence, but he didn't need to lose his daughter.

Relief made Zoey feel tons lighter. She hadn't fallen for a child abuser. He was just what he appeared to be, no matter what any grieving in-laws or professional reports claimed.

Jessy, she knew without a doubt, was lucky to have him.

And no matter what it meant to her, Zoey knew she couldn't jeopardize that.

Chapter Eight

"Are you comin' home over my house today?" Jessy asked as Dillon stopped the car in front of the Whites' house late the next afternoon.

"No, sweetheart, you know I can't come in with you."

"Please." Her bottom lip was starting to quiver.

"How about a piggyback ride up to the door?" Dillon offered, pretending enthusiasm to hide that he felt as sad as his daughter looked every time he had to leave her here.

"I doan wanna go," Jessy informed him, her eyes filling. "I wanna stay with you, Dad."

"I know, baby. But you can't stay with me. You have to go inside." He took her out of the car seat and carried her to the front door. "Please don't do this, Jess," he whispered into her hair when he'd pushed the doorbell and she clamped her arms around his neck like a vise.

"I wanna stay with you, Dad," she repeated tearfully.

The door opened just then and surprise made Dillon forget to answer his daughter. For the first time since the custody battle had begun he looked straight into the time-lined face of his father-in-law.

Richard White didn't smile, neither did Dillon. "Evelyn and I would like a few words with you, if you have the time."

A rush of anger suddenly shot through Dillon. Grief or no grief, this man and his wife didn't have the right to put Jessy and him through what they had. It was on the tip of his tongue to tell the old man to talk to his attorney, turn around and take Jessy home. Let them break down his damn door to get to her.

But Dillon's better judgment and a dozen warnings from Frank against doing anything that made him look irrational, kept him where he was. Instead he just glared at Richard White, eye to eye.

Nearly sixty-two, his father-in-law had been treated kindly by time. He was lean and strong and still distinguished-looking. Dillon remembered the innumerable golf games and tennis matches they'd played. They had also shared laughs, bets, conspiracies. He didn't know where the memory had come from, but there it was—he'd thought of Richard as more than his father-in-law. He'd thought of him as his friend. "All right, I'll come in," he agreed tightly.

The gray-haired man stepped aside and Dillon went into the dark oak-paneled foyer. It smelled the same as it had the first time he'd ever set foot in this place—old wood and lemon. He hadn't been nervous about meeting Linda's parents. Everything she'd said about them had made them sound like nice, ordinary people. And over the years that was how he'd found both of them to be.

"Marge will take Jessy to her room," the older man said matter-of-factly.

"I doan wan Marge. She gits mad to me when I say bad words," Jessy cried as the maid stepped from the shadows of the staircase, which faced the door.

"It's okay, sweetheart," Dillon soothed, all the while keeping his eyes on his father-in-law.

But it wasn't okay with Jessy, and as always the maid had to pry the little girl out of her father's arms.

"Evelyn is in the living room," Richard informed him over Jessy's cries, which were fading as the maid carried her farther up the stairs.

How could you have done this? Dillon thought. *And how can you see that I'm the one she she wants, that I'm the one she's calling for and keep this up?* But he only inclined his head slightly and entered through the double entrance to his left.

Evelyn White sat on a brocade sofa, her long legs crossed, her beringed hands idly in her lap. Her striking blond hair was chin-length and fashionable, as was the pantsuit she wore. All in all, she looked much younger than her fifty-nine years and for the first time in a long while Dillon had a vivid flash of Linda, who had looked a great deal like her mother. He had once thought that he'd be happy to have a wife who aged like Evelyn.

The fact that she smiled at him made Dillon wonder if the hatchet was about to be buried. He'd listen to anything they wanted to say, if it meant walking out of this place with Jessy in his arms.

"Evelyn," he greeted his former mother-in-law.

"Please sit down, Dillon," she said as her husband took his place beside her.

Dillon sat across from them in a wing chair, settling back as if nothing had changed since he'd last visited them two days before the accident, when they had all been on good terms.

Richard began. "We wanted to give you a last chance to come to your senses before the court date and more hard feelings are raised," he said with only the trace of a threat in his tone.

So much for burying the hatchet. Dillon couldn't help the mirthless laugh that answered the older man.

"We were hoping that you might relinquish Jessy to us without going through the hearing. In return we'll agree to generous visitation," Evelyn put in, as if she was offering him a piece of pie.

Dillon shook his head, slowly, ruefully. "No."

"Think about it, Dillon," Evelyn cautioned.

"No, I won't. Jessy is my daughter and I'm going to raise her. There's nothing else to think about."

"You never were short on confidence," Richard put in. "But this time it could be a mistake."

Where had the hostility come from? Dillon wondered. Before this had all begun he'd been sure the three of them would remain close, all of them only wanting what was best for Jessy. "I don't know what kind of a case you think you have. What I do know is that there isn't a damn reason in the world why I shouldn't be granted custody. And I think you know it, or else why this last-minute effort to get me to give her up?"

"We don't want to hurt you, Dillon," Evelyn said. "But we'll do whatever we have to, to ensure that Jessica is raised the way she should be."

"This 'last-minute effort,' as you put it," Richard went on, "is our way of trying to spare you, believe it or not. You aren't going to win this."

Dillon stared at the other man for a moment. "I guess we'll see, won't we?"

"Don't make us use what the detective has found," Evelyn implored quietly.

"Detective?" The word didn't ring true.

"We've had you investigated," Richard informed him. "Complete with photographs of last week's visit taken by your neighbor to substantiate that being with you isn't in Jessica's best interest."

Photographs taken by a neighbor? That one knocked Dillon off his pins for a moment before he realized his father-in-law was still talking.

"If you let this go to court we'll expose those pictures

and not only will they win us the case, but they will probably get your visitation significantly reduced and limited, if not disallowed completely."

"It would be better all the way around if we could come to an agreement ourselves," Evelyn finished.

"You had me investigated?"

"Substantially," Richard said.

"And what the hell did you have photographed?"

"Everything. Morning, noon and night," Richard answered.

"By a neighbor who could see almost everything that went on in your house," Evelyn put in.

"Who happens to be a *professional* photographer," the older man finished.

Zoey? "I don't believe it."

"No matter what contemporary opinion holds, I know what's involved in raising a child, particularly a daughter," Evelyn asserted. "And a single man alone can't do it. At least, not well. If you really love Jessica you would want the best for her."

"Think of yourself, too, Dillon." Richard was obviously trying a new tack, complete with the tone of voice Dillon remembered well and had always considered companionable. Until now. "You're still young. You need to go on with your life. That means other women in your house at all hours, you at theirs. We understand that and don't begrudge you, believe me. But it's no environment for a little girl."

"I've already had my adolescence, thank you very much. I don't need a second round. And regardless of what you imagine, I can actually have a social life *and* raise my daughter in a wholesome environment." Dillon stood. "I'll take my chances in court. Even against your investigator and your pictures."

His in-laws didn't say anything as he walked out without giving them a backward glance. He very nearly didn't give them a second thought, either, as he started his car and drove off their property. Of all the things they'd said there was only one that stayed with him, ringing in his ears.

Was it really possible that Zoey had spent last week taking pictures of him and Jess?

It wasn't. It couldn't be. He couldn't believe it. It took somebody pretty low to do a thing like that. And she hadn't even been around most of the time.

Or had she? She'd been married to Carl Carmichael, a wildlife photographer renowned for canny hiding abilities that had allowed him to produce close-up, candid shots of the most skittish of wild animals. She'd spent seven years with him in Africa. Surely she knew the best of his tricks. Had she been putting them to work just last week? And then spent the weekend with him?

What kind of a person would do something like that? Someone cold and calculating. Someone who was a liar and a sneak. Zoey? As Mata Hari? Not likely.

But he couldn't get the Whites' words out of his mind. *Photographs taken by your neighbor...who could see almost everything that went on in the house...who happens to be a professional photographer.*

A lot of people could probably see into his house. But as far as Dillon knew, he didn't have any other neighbor who was a professional photographer.

"So maybe there's one that I don't know," he offered himself as he merged onto the Boulder Turnpike.

But he had to admit that it didn't seem likely. And yet he just couldn't buy Zoey working for some private investigator and taking hidden-camera pictures of him.

"She'd have to have had a damn good reason," he reassured himself.

But what reason could be good enough?

Harold Miflin knew what he was talking about, Zoey thought at four-thirty that Tuesday afternoon as she hung up her phone. And he hadn't been bluffing. The subpoena had been served an hour before. She had called the attorney who had handled all of Carl's legal affairs to confirm the consequences of not complying with it—fines and a stay in jail until she did turn over those pictures. Just what Miflin had threatened.

With a shriek of frustration she charged the trampoline, climbed up and jumped so hard that her knees buckled. She fell flat on her face.

Dammit all.

Spread-eagle, she stayed there, with her nose and forehead pressed into the mat. "I'll just have to go to jail."

Hearing her own words struck her and Zoey rolled to her back, arms and legs splayed, and stared at the ceiling. Had she just said that?

"I'm in trouble," she whispered. And not only because of what could happen to her if she ignored the subpoena. A sure sign of her loving someone was her being ready to throw herself into the flames for that person. And going to jail definitely qualified as the flames.

She did love Dillon, she admitted. She didn't want to, but she did. And she couldn't think about it now, when there was so much else on her mind. Later she'd have to consider what she'd let herself in for emotionally. But right now figuring out what to do with those snapshots had to be the first priority.

What *was* she going to do with them? Or better yet, what *could* she do with them?

There weren't a lot of answers because there weren't a lot of choices. Hand the snapshots over to Miflin, watch Dillon lose Jessy, and save her own butt. Or not hand them over and go to jail.

She didn't really need to think about it, she realized. The answer was a simple one. Cut-and-dried. Because there was no alternative. She couldn't be a part of taking Jessy away from Dillon. Not for Dillon's sake and not for Jessy's. The two of them and their relationship for the rest of their lives couldn't be sacrificed to keep her rear end out of the wringer. That was all there was to it.

"Guess I can be the official resident prison photographer," she said ruefully to her ceiling.

Then it occurred to her that there was one thing jail would accomplish. It would keep her away from Dillon and the trap he represented to her. And that might save her from herself and these feelings she should never have let go this far.

That evening Dillon called after five about dinner. He didn't sound like himself. There was no teasing, no light-hearted fun on the phone, but Zoey didn't think much of it.

He picked her up an hour later and they decided on a Mexican restaurant a few blocks away. She had never seen him so quiet.

"Is everything okay?" she asked as they got out of the car in the parking lot.

He opened her door. "Sure. Why?"

"You just seem kind of down."

He shrugged. Zoey waited for more of a response but he merely took her elbow and went into the restaurant without saying anything else.

"I know it's hard for you to bring Jessy back to her grandparents," she said as they were seated, guessing that as the cause for his mood.

His blue eyes seemed to bore into her for a moment before he agreed. "It's real hard."

They read their menus in silence.

Should she confess what she'd done? she wondered, rather than paying much attention to what she wanted for dinner. Should she warn him about what was going on behind his back?

She should. But somehow when the waitress had taken their order and left them alone, the questioning frown that she met on Dillon's face kept her quiet. This didn't seem like a good time and so she put it off. She would tell him. But not right now.

Then Dillon broke the silence. "So. How's the photography business?"

"As a matter of fact I got an account just yesterday that should keep the wolves at bay. And I have an important meeting tomorrow at ten with the bigger departments of the same store. If I cage them, too, it could actually put me in the pink. Or is that the black?" she tried to make a joke.

He didn't seem to catch it. "I didn't know the wolves were baying."

It was Zoey's turn to shrug. "I've been out of circulation for a long time and just putting a sign up doesn't do much. This month was a first for me—I had bills I couldn't cover. I had to let my medical insurance lapse."

Their meal was served and Zoey went on when the waitress left. "Anyway, it doesn't matter now. I got an advance on the Mayco account. I mailed the check to reactivate my insurance today."

"I assumed your husband had left you some security."

Zoey told him about their agreement to donate the estate to the wildlife foundation. "Don't look so worried," she said, laughing at his expression even as she appreciated his concern. "Just keep your fingers crossed that I get the rest of Mayco's business."

"Is this the first job you've had since you've been back?"

Zoey choked on a bit of particularly hot green chili. "One of them," she answered vaguely when she could. Then she changed the subject. "How about you? Is there another hair-raising roller-coaster ride on your drawing board?"

He shrugged and pushed his only half-eaten burrito away. "I had some proposals in to Fun City. They're looking at adding several new rides when they move into central Denver. They called this afternoon to say they were buying."

"Congratulations! I'd think that would have made you happy."

"I'm glad. But my priority right now is Jessy."

Zoey realized she didn't have much of an appetite, either, and let the waitress remove what was left of her meal, as well. "It's good for that, too, though, isn't it? It means you can work right here in Denver for a long time." She was thinking about his traveling being a bone of contention in the custody suit.

"I was going to stay here for a long time, one way or another. I've already put an ad in the papers for an assistant who's willing to travel."

"Terrific." The word had come out a little too enthusiastically.

Dillon paid their tab and held her chair as she stood. On the way out Zoey realized what a quick meal it had been, when she saw their waitress just serving a couple who had been seated shortly after she and Dillon.

"Did Jessy put up an unusually bad battle about your leaving her today?" she asked as he opened the car door for her, hoping that if she could get him to talk about it it might help both him and his mood.

"She cried and hung on to me, but actually it was cut shorter than usual."

Maybe that was the problem. Maybe he was worried that he was losing ground in his daughter's affections. She waited for him to get in behind the steering wheel, start the car and pull out of the parking lot. "You know, she's lucky to have you."

He stared at her for a moment. "You think so?"

"Yes, I do. My own father worked two jobs the whole time we were all growing up, so he wasn't around much. But even when he was, he never changed a diaper or gave a bath or washed a head of hair. Until I was old enough to do it, if my mother had to go somewhere she had her sister come over and take care of us and the house and him until she got back. When I was old enough and she'd leave, I'd do everything, including waiting on my father the way she did. He never read a bedtime story and he certainly never took any of us to the zoo or played with us the way you do with Jessy.''

''Then your father missed out on a lot.''

Zoey smiled at him. ''He didn't think so. But I really admire that you feel that way. Like I said, she's lucky to have you.''

He frowned. ''That only occurs to me in the reverse—that I'm lucky to have her.''

''You are. But don't overlook all you give her in return.''

He pulled the car to a stop in front of her house and switched off the engine. Then he turned toward her, stretching his arm along the back of the seat to toy with her hair. The smile he sent her way was still not his usual, but it was closer than he'd come all evening. It felt good to know she could help even a little with his problems.

''Am I invited in?'' he asked.

''Of course.''

But he didn't move right away and as he sat staring at her she studied him in return, reveling in the sight of his face—lean and angular and strikingly handsome. It seemed suddenly strange to her that she had ever doubted him. There was no artifice about him. He was honest, gentle, kind, giving, sensitive, strong. He was a man so secure in his own masculinity that he didn't need to hide his softer side. No wonder he was so appealing, so attractive, so sexy. And it amazed her to realize how strong the power of suggestion was. It had thrown up a smoke screen in front of all that was good and desirable about Dillon.

He finally got out of the car. Zoey didn't wait for him to come around to her side. Instead she got out, too, and led the way up to her house. ''There's still some of the wine from Sunday night. Would you like a glass?'' she asked as they went inside.

''What I'd really like is to turn the lights off and just sit and hold you.''

His mood was still odd, but his request would get no complaints from her. ''You're easy to please.''

He sat at one end of the couch and reached up to turn off the lamp. The moon was full and low in the sky, casting a snowy glow through the big picture window.

Zoey joined him and when she didn't sit as close as he wanted, he pulled her back against his chest, locking his arms around her. The scent of his after-shave drifted down and his breath was warm against her ear as he bent to kiss it.

"You never answered me when I asked you the other night what you wanted in your future besides your business," he said in a deep, soft voice.

Him, was the first thing that came to mind, she wanted him. But that was dangerous territory, so she only shrugged and fought the temptation to tell him how she felt about him.

When she didn't answer he went on, "I know I said you didn't have to say anything when I told you I love you. But I can't help wondering how you feel about me... besides scared."

Would it be so awful to tell him the truth? she asked herself. After all, admitting her feelings didn't make a commitment, nor was he asking for one. It was just a declaration. And one that might ease what was troubling him, as well as help him to believe, when the time came to explain that she hadn't taken Miflin's job to hurt anyone.

"I'd sworn off," she began. "I needed...need...time to only be responsible for myself, to put myself first, to concentrate on getting my business back in gear. But the feelings didn't wait their turn on the timetable." She paused. "I love you, Dillon."

"I want to believe that," he said so softly she wasn't sure if she was meant to hear it. She hoped he was teasing, even though it didn't sound like it.

"It's true." She craned her head back to look up into his face, so handsome, so solemn tonight. "I do love you."

He smiled then, a slow, warm smile that set her insides dancing. "I love you, too, Zoey," he answered with such sincerity she felt reassured that his quiet mood had nothing to do with their relationship.

He kissed her then, his lips parted, moist and seeking. As his mouth enticed hers, his hands slid up to her breasts, finding both at once in a touch that was tender and demanding at the same time. Her thin silk blouse seemed like armor separating his hands from her instantly passion-aroused nipples.

As if he knew, Dillon lifted her onto his lap where his own craving for her was already a hard ridge within his khaki slacks. He made short work of her buttons, slipping his hand inside her shirt to find that tonight she had been daring and worn nothing underneath.

Zoey rubbed against him as she wrapped her arms around his neck. Then he released her breasts and carried her to bed. He laid her on the quilt and joined her, throwing his sinewy thigh across hers as if she might try to leave.

But there was nowhere else in the world Zoey wanted to be. She toyed with his hair where it waved against his nape, reveling in the feel of the straining cords of his neck as he took her mouth again and found her tongue with his. He seemed to be questioning if she was feeling the same ever building need he was.

With one hand he slid her blouse off her shoulders. Short, urgent kisses trailed down her neck to the hollow of her throat and then lower, to the valley between her breasts, his tongue flicking there in a sensual torment.

Zoey took a deep breath that made her breasts rise, and announced her own needs, making him chuckle only slightly before taking one straining crest fully into his mouth. Again his tongue worked, flicking, circling, stroking in a slow, rhythmic velvet caress.

He unfastened her pants and slipped off everything at once, leaving her naked. Impatiently Zoey made short work of his clothes, for the second time finding him without anything underneath his slacks. Then she explored. A broad shoulder, as far as she could reach around his wide back, a firm side and then a hard pectoral and nipple. She flattened her palm down his rib cage and found his hip, then his derriere, as tight to the touch as it was to look at.

Dillon tensed, sending her a message that said it was time she grew brave enough to touch him the way he did her. And Zoey was ready. No, not just ready, she was anxious.

Slowly she drew her hand around, stopping just short of the juncture of his legs to torture him. He groaned a complaint at her breast and she smiled.

Pressing her palm along the lowest part of his abdomen, she made her way to his center and finally found him, long and thick and hard and powerful. Closing her hand around him made his whole body stiffen, as if the pleasure she had sent through him was almost more than she could stand.

Zoey thought that his response to her touch was one of the most arousing things he had done. Until he spread her thighs and found those corresponding parts of her own. Then it was she who stiffened and arched as if lightning bolts had struck inside her, one shooting downward from his sudden tender nip of her breast, the other upward from the tip of the finger he slipped inside her. His palm cupped her tightly and rocked rhythmically against the slight mound between her legs. She couldn't help arching up into it even more, all the while keeping hold of him and working a little magic of her own until they were both in a frenzy of need.

He rolled her to her back then, rose above her and came into her in one movement that joined them as perfectly as if they were a matched set. He kissed her, once, twice, pulsing inside her each time, so deeply, so sweetly, that her back was pulled up off the mattress.

Gradually he began, his hips circling in a way that made him delve into her and then move out, again and again, so steadily it was easy for Zoey to answer the same way. But passion demanded more and Dillon seemed only too willing to give it. Faster, harder, deeper, he thrust into her, sending tidal waves of pleasure all through her until all she could

do was ride it to its climax, clinging to him, arching up
into him, wrapping her legs around him, only peripherally
aware that he, too, had found his own peak almost at the
same time.

And then slowly, slowly, both crescendos ebbed. Tightened muscles eased, just a little at a time, leaving them in
unequaled tranquility.

"I love you, Zoey," he whispered hoarsely.

"Oh, Dillon, I love you," she answered without compunction.

Then he rolled them to their sides, still deeply embedded
inside her, and held her tightly against the long, hard length
of him.

Zoey felt weighted but in the most marvelous way, liq-
uid, lazy, languid. In the moment just before she fell asleep,
she had the sense that Dillon had kept them together in
answer to his own need to feel that what was between them
was more than just sexual, a need for a deeper bonding of
their hearts and spirits, a need for that to soothe his sadness
over leaving his daughter today. But he hadn't been the
only one of them to need something. Zoey had needed reassurance that he did love her, that he would understand
what she had to tell him, and that just maybe it would help
cushion the blow.

Chapter Nine

Dillon's suspicions that Zoey had secretly photographed him and Jessy had begun to dissipate when she told him Jessy was lucky to have him as her father. The words and sentiment had rung true. Then she'd said she loved him, and believing she couldn't have done anything that would hurt his chances at regaining custody of Jessy had felt all the more right. They had made love and Dillon had told himself his suspicions of her had been unfounded. He didn't know what it was, but he was convinced that there was another explanation for all of this. He'd gone to sleep a happy man.

Then he had dreamed about his meeting with his in-laws. Only in this version Zoey was sitting on the couch between them, the whole time fiddling with her camera and snapping a picture of him every time she thought he wasn't looking.

When he woke up at six, suspicion—unwelcome and ugly—was back in full force.

He crossed his hands under his head and looked out the

picture window at the other end of the house. The sun was just rising in a bare hint of butter yellow and bursts of pink lemonade. But today the sight didn't impress him.

Sometime during the night Zoey had rolled to the other side of the bed and turned her back on him. The last time she had stayed in his arms. He couldn't help wondering if her conscience was ruling her sleep.

Dillon eased up and leaned against the brass head rail, using his pillow for padding. But it wasn't the sunrise he looked at. It was Zoey's studio, just off the foot of the bed.

Backdrop screens were hung on the side wall. A tripod was positioned more than halfway to the kitchen's island counter. Low cupboards, shelves and a filing cabinet partitioned it from the living room on one side and the bedroom on the other. There was an assortment of props and gadgets he wasn't familiar with, and lights and big umbrellas that he assumed helped her to control glares and glows.

As he took it all in, Dillon wished he could find some comfort in the evidence that she was a studio photographer. But knowing she had been married to Carl Carmichael prevented it. Her forte might be still pictures that were composed and positioned ahead of time, but surely she had a good deal of knowledge about the more candid kind of photography. The kind that her husband had practiced. The kind that would have made her capable of hiding herself while taking snapshots through the back glass wall of his house.

He turned his head and looked at her beside him. Her wavy hair fanned out his way and he couldn't resist reaching for a strand.

Why the hell would you do it?

She must not have been sleeping too soundly because that bare touch of her hair disturbed her. She rolled over onto her back and looked up at him as if she had been awake all along. "What are you doing up so early?"

What should he say? *I was trying to figure out how you*

*could spy on me for the enemy and then let me make love
to you? Or, I couldn't sleep for wondering where in this
simple place you've hidden pictures that people want to
use to keep my daughter away from me?*

So instead he shrugged and said, "I woke up." But it
came out surly and made her frown.

"What's wrong, Dillon?" she asked.

Was that genuine concern in her voice? How could it be
if she had done this?

For a moment he just stared at her face and those pale
seafoam-green eyes of hers. Then he forced himself to look
straight ahead and tell her what was on his mind. "Yesterday when I took Jessy back to the Whites, Richard asked
me in. He and Evelyn wanted to give me one last chance
to give up Jessy before the whole thing goes to court and
gets uglier." He waited but she didn't say anything.
"Seems they hired a detective who hired a professional
photographer to play spy last week, and now they have
pictures to prove what an unfit father I am."

The words dropped like lead and left nothing but silence.
Dillon looked at Zoey, willing her to deny that she was the
photographer. But instead she got out of bed.

His gaze went from her bare, thin, straight back, down
to her narrow, tight rear end as she headed for the closet.
A memory flashed into his mind—his hands splayed against
that backside, holding her hips up just before he'd pressed
inside her. He clenched his teeth against the desire that
came so easily, and stared at her shoulders instead as she
opened a door and took a plain white robe from a hook.
He couldn't deny that there were other things he would
rather be doing than accusing her of something he wasn't
sure he could forgive. Still facing away from him, she
shrugged into the robe and tied it around her waist.

*Turn around and tell me I'm a bastard for thinking you
would do something like this.*

But she didn't turn around. She went into the studio section, straight to the filing cabinet. And then she came back to bed, carrying a bulging folder.

"They don't have the pictures," she said softly. "I do. I'm the photographer."

Dillon just stared at her, still not completely believing it.

"The investigator's name is Harold Miflin. He came to my door the morning after our Sunday at the zoo to hire me."

Dillon shook his head in denial. "Where have I heard that name?"

"Monday morning on my answering machine," she responded flatly.

"*He* was your business meeting?"

She grimaced. "Don't sound so disillusioned."

He raked his fingers through his hair, trying to absorb what she was saying. There had to be a good explanation. "I think you'd better give me the whole story."

She sat on the very edge of the bed, far away from him, but she looked him in the eye. "I barely knew you when Miflin came to hire me," she reminded him. "But even then I wasn't crazy about the job."

"Then why did you take it?" he asked without accusation. "I know money was tight and you were worried about it, but there must have been something else you could have done."

"The money was an issue when he first showed up. I just thought he was a prospective client, and I needed the work. But after he'd told me what the job was, being paid didn't enter into my decision. I took it because I couldn't refuse when I thought Jessy might be in some danger, in spite of what I thought about you, in spite of the attraction..." she trailed off.

Dillon breathed a short, unhappy laugh. In all he'd thought, that hadn't occurred to him. Probably because he never thought of Jessy as being in danger. "I guess I can understand that. I wouldn't want anybody to close his eyes to a situation that looked like a child was being abused."

He spanned his forehead with one hand and pressed each temple before meeting her searching glance. "But I have to tell you I'm a little confused about what made you think that was Jessy's situation."

"There were a lot of reasons. Finding Jessy in my yard by herself, your not being too conscientious about what she ate, and my having to suggest and then oversee adding safer locks. It all seemed alarming, when Miflin told me Jessy had already been taken away from you."

He lost his grip on his patience. "Taken away from me? She wasn't taken away from me. And for crying out loud, Zoey, do you honestly think that without you I wouldn't have taken measures to keep her from unlocking the doors again? It only happened a second time because I didn't believe the sitter. And the sole reason I put the damn locks up while you were there was as a joke, because you were playing mother hen. I figured it would put your mind to rest."

"I know now that Jessy wasn't taken away from you, but I didn't until you told me. Miflin made it sound like you had already been found unfit. He also led me to believe that he was an investigator for the court. I didn't know until Monday morning that your in-laws are who he works for."

Dillon shook his head. "This is incredible."

"It gets worse."

As he listened, she told him about her Monday morning meeting in Miflin's office. When she was finished he felt a little numb. "Doctors and psychologists? That's crazy. The Whites wouldn't go so far as to pay off professionals."

"You think they paid for those reports?"

"There's no other way they could have gotten them."

"But Dillon..." She stopped and looked down at the file folder in her lap.

"What?"

"It's just that some of it is true. And the pictures show it. Your house is dangerous and you don't feed her well and..."

"And I seem irresponsible to you, is that it?" He frowned at her, surprised.

"Not irresponsible. Just inexperienced. And in need of having your eyes opened, and a little guidance."

"Having my eyes opened and a little guidance?" He didn't know whether to laugh or be mad at her. "You're right as far as inexperience goes. I haven't had much on-the-job training, and until recently I didn't have any idea to what extent a house had to be kidproofed. But I'm not blind, Zoey. Last week with Jessy let me know in a big way that some things had to be changed. And that's all there is to it, regardless of what I'm being accused of. I don't need to have my eyes opened and I don't need guidance. And I'm sure as hell not negligent."

"I didn't say you were. At least not in any way but by oversight."

Still he heard doubt in her voice. He swung his legs to the floor and pulled on his pants. Then he stood, rounded the bed, took the file folder out of her hands and laid them on the mattress. He pulled Zoey up. "Come on, Carmichael. I have some things to show you."

She didn't say anything and he didn't look back as he led her by the hand up to his house. After taking his keys out of his pants pocket, Dillon opened the sliding-glass door and headed straight through the kitchen into the living room where there were three sacks on the couch. Only then did he let go of Zoey's hand to spill the sacks' contents in the center of the floor.

"Exhibited for your approval and peace of mind, Carmichael. Not only the best, but *everything* Baby World sells in the way of safety gadgets. I went shopping Monday morning and had plans for using the time between now and the hearing to install it all. And—" he reached for some books that were buried underneath "—if you'll remember, I also told you I needed to learn to cook. See, proof that I'm earnest—a cookbook any moron could work from, one on how to make food even the pickiest kid will eat, and a guide to children's nutritional needs. Yes, I indulged her finicky eating habits last week. It was like a vacation for us both, and everything goes a little lax on vacation. It was a rotten week to put me under a microscope. But believe me, once I have permanent custody I defy any supermom alive to find fault.''

Dillon watched Zoey stare at the pile of cupboard latches, grates, outlet plugs, tub accessories, childproof appliance locks and a dozen other things he'd yet to figure out. Suddenly she gave a breathless little chuckle. "I don't believe this. I've never seen half this stuff. You're going to turn the place into Fort Knox.''

"At least," Dillon assured her.

"And I'll have to slip her a piece of candy every now and then, just so she remembers what sugar tastes like.''

"So long as it's not too often.''

"You really were aware of the problems," she marveled.

"Of course I was.''

"Then why did it take until last week for you to realize you needed this stuff?''

"Why would I have realized it before? Jessy is my first and only child, remember? And since she was six months old, I've never had her with me for more than an afternoon at a time.''

"But I assumed... How could a doctor and a psychologist find so many effects after only a few hours?''

"Exactly. Like I said, my in-laws must have paid for those reports. Maybe this handy detective has some kind of connections.''

The color drained from her face. "Then the photographs could confirm false reports.''

"I think we better go back to your place and take a look at those pictures.''

This time Zoey led the way. As they both sat on the edge of her bed, she handed him several snapshots at once, pointing out those that she thought gave a negative impression. It didn't make Dillon feel any better to realize she was

right. If he were making a judgment based on them he'd
be hesitant to put a child under the kind of care that found
her hanging from a second-floor railing and eating out of
a trash basket.

He tossed the last one back into the open folder and
pinched the bridge of his nose.

"You don't need to worry about it," she said then, quietly. "I've already decided not to comply with the subpoena."

"Subpoena?" The situation was getting worse by the
minute.

She answered him stiltedly, stalling between words.
"When I didn't bring the pictures to Miflin, Monday, he
had your in-laws' lawyer subpoena them."

"And you've already been served?"

"Late yesterday afternoon," she confirmed. Then she
went on in a rush. "But that doesn't change anything. I
honestly had already decided not to give Miflin the pictures,
to ignore it."

"To ignore a subpoena?" he reiterated, his disbelief
mounting again. "I'm not the lawyer in the family, but I
know enough to realize that you can't just ignore a subpoena. Do you think I want to win this damn case at your
expense?"

"Do you think I want you to lose it because of me?"
she countered. "It's my choice, Dillon."

"Taking the job was your choice. But we're in this part
of it together now." He grabbed his shirt and slipped it
over his head. "I have to get hold of Frank and see where
we both stand. I don't want to call. Maybe I'm being para-
noid, but if the Whites went so far as to hire a private
detective, who knows if phones are bugged, too." He
brushed soil off the bottom of his feet and put on his shoes
and shocks. Then he turned to look at her again. "In the
meantime, don't do anything at all."

Something about her expression made him think she was

silently disagreeing with him. "On second thought, maybe you should come with me."

She cringed at that idea. "No thanks. Confessing this to you has been bad enough. I'd rather not take on your brother, the lawyer, too. You can break the news to him. It isn't as if I expect the police at my door any minute."

He stared at her for a moment and then sighed. "All right, Zoey, but I don't want you to answer the door to anyone but me, just in case. Close your drapes and if someone knocks or rings the bell hide in the darkroom. Got that?"

She nodded, but he still wasn't convinced she was agreeing with him. "I mean it, Zoey. Don't do anything until I get back with Frank's advice."

She nodded again, as weakly as the first. But Dillon didn't have the time to press his point. He kissed her once more and nearly ran out of her house, hoping his brother knew a legal loophole that could get them out of this.

When the door closed behind Dillon, Zoey toppled over onto the mattress. She wished she could bury her head under her pillow and never come out.

"Coward," she called herself.

At least Dillon hadn't taken the news that she was his in-laws' photographer too badly. Unfortunately that didn't assuage the guilt she felt. Especially since she'd found out he really was aware of all that needed to be done to make his house safer for Jessy and had put the wheels in motion. In fact it made her feel worse that Dillon really was a conscientious father and she might have contributed to the lies against him. If anyone ever got hold of those pictures...

Zoey sat up in a hurry.

What if somehow those pictures ever did get out? Just refusing to turn them over might not be enough. What if she was put in jail and then a search warrant was issued, allowing the police to come in here, find them and use them anyway?

"Am I being melodramatic?" she wondered out loud. All she knew about the law was what she had seen on TV and what she had asked Carl's attorney after the subpoena had been served. Since this had just occurred to her, it hadn't been on her list of questions. But it seemed possible. And how could she take that kind of chance?

As if Dillon was in the room with her, she heard his parting words again, those that had ordered her not to do anything until he got back. Should she wait? And what would happen if she did? Wouldn't Dillon be loathe to do anything that might jeopardize her? He'd said he didn't want to win at her expense. She thought he would try to protect her even if it complicated his case. But this was her responsibility. She had caused it and she had to fix it.

Zoey scooped all the pictures back into the file folder. Then she got off the bed and went out onto the back patio. Her barbecue grill was just big enough for four hamburgers or two steaks and barely as tall as her knees. She brought it in and set it in the center of the room. Then she went for matches, newspaper and the bulging file.

It felt good to be doing something. To be taking control of the situation. Harold Miflin and the Whites and the court could find her and penalize her and put her in jail. But there was no way any of them would be able to resurrect those pictures and use them against Dillon.

She took the grill off, wadded several pages of newspaper and set them in the fire bowl. Then she struck a match and lit the paper. Kneeling beside the flames, she opened the file, picked up the picture that made it look as if Arachnid was about to take a bloody chunk out of Jessy, and placed it on top of the pile. Within seconds the edges curled and the incriminating photo disappeared.

The relief she felt watching it convinced Zoey she was doing the right thing. One by one she burned her work, not adding another snapshot until she was sure the previous one had disintegrated into ashes.

But the seventh picture caught her eye and she paused

to look at it. Dillon sat in the rocking chair in Jessy's bedroom, holding the little girl who was snuggled against his chest as he read to her.

"Too bad the court doesn't see this," she murmured.

She stretched her arm to add it to the fire when something occurred to her and she stopped short. If the pictures that made Dillon look like an exemplary parent were submitted, wouldn't they go a long way in convincing the court that he was a good father?

There was no doubt about it. The good ones were very moving. In the face of them, no one could deny that Jessy should be raised by Dillon. And not only that—it would mean she was almost complying with the subpoena.

Quickly she sorted through what remained of the photographs and then did the same with the negatives, burning everything that didn't make Dillon look like an ideal parent. While the last of them curled into ashes she very meticulously sorted those she had kept, clipping the corresponding negatives to the corner of every picture. When that was finished and they were all neatly back in the file folder she got dressed.

"Wish me luck," she said to no one in particular on her way out of the house. "We have to hope that Harold Miflin isn't much for paying attention to details."

Chapter Ten

Frank was just leaving when Dillon pulled up in front of his house. "Isn't this early for you?" Dillon called to his brother as he crossed from the curb to the driveway where Frank stood beside the open door of his car. "I expected to have to wake you up."

"I have an early deposition." Frank pointed his chin at Dillon. "You look like you just rolled out of bed."

"Just about," he confirmed, propping himself against the front fender with one hip and resting his arm on the rooftop.

"What's up?"

"There's a few new developments on the custody front. I need to know how much trouble I'm in and where to go from here."

Frank frowned. "Okay. But if it's a long story I'm going to need the condensed version. I don't have much time."

"Then I won't waste any." Dillon explained all he knew about the pictures and what Zoey had told him about the Whites' case against him. As the whole thing unfolded he watched his brother's expression turn more grim. "I knew this wasn't good when I came over here, but by the look on your face you're going to tell me it's even worse than I thought, aren't you?" he said when he'd finished.

Frank's cheeks puffed and he blew them out. "It's definitely not good."

Dillon nodded, realizing just then how much he had been counting on Frank being able to give him an easy solution, in spite of knowing that there wasn't going to be one. "Lay it out for me," he prompted.

"You don't need me to tell you that doctors and shrinks can carry a lot of weight in cases like this, and proving your theory that they were paid to say what the Whites wanted isn't easy. Add pictures that don't make you look like a sterling parent and we could be facing some big-time trouble. What kind of a person is this neighbor of yours, anyway?" Frank finished derisively.

"Not as bad as this makes her sound," Dillon defended.

"The woman took pictures of you through your windows to help your in-laws keep Jessy. How can that sound anything but bad?"

Dillon shook his head. "Until the other night I hadn't told her anything, at all. The detective made her think he was working for the court. He came off like an unbiased investigator just looking for the facts, but he insinuated that Jessy had been taken away from me because the court had already found me unfit. She thought that if she didn't take the job she might be looking the other way while Jess was abused. She's the kind of person who couldn't and wouldn't do that. As much as it's messed up this already messed-up situation, I wouldn't want someone who was confronted with possible child abuse and didn't do what she could to help."

Frank looked at him through wide eyes. "Okay, okay. Don't bite my head off."

Dillon raised his hands. "Sorry. I'm a little on edge and this woman means a lot to me."

"Great. So you've fallen head over heels for someone who isn't afraid to get involved. Ordinarily I'd say that was terrific. The trouble is, her getting involved has done you damage."

"That's why I'm here, counselor, so you can fix it. The pictures have been subpoenaed and she's decided not to comply—"

"Score one for our side."

"You didn't let me finish. I want you to do something that pulls me out of the fire without putting her in it, Frank. I don't want her going to jail for contempt of court."

His brother shook his head and sighed. "What you want is a miracle, Dillon. Do I look anything like a miracle worker to you?"

"Sure."

"Well, look again. There's nothing I can do. She hands the pictures over, or else. And if she hands them over... well, we're going to have our work cut out for us just going up against doctors and shrinks. The last thing we need are pictures of Jessy swinging from the rafters with you no-where in sight."

"So what are you saying? That I should let Zoey refuse to comply and go to jail?"

"I might be able to get her out within a day or so. But if you lose this case there's a chance you'll never get Jessy back."

Dillon pressed his temples against the headache that was beginning to pound there.

"I'm sorry, Dil," Frank said. "I wish I could tell you something else, because I know you really care for this woman. But the choice is her or Jessy. Pick one, sacrifice the other."

Dillon glared at him. "Dammit, I'm a good father," he ground out through clenched teeth. "Why should I have to feed Zoey to the gods in order to raise my own daughter?"

"You're right, it stinks. And you don't have to tell me you're a good father. I know it and I'm not undervaluing it. The truth is our biggest asset. But I have to tell you what you're up against, don't I?''

"That's what I asked for," Dillon admitted sardonically.

Frank glanced at his watch. "Look, I have to get going. Call me later today and let me know what's happening, will you?"

"Sure," Dillon answered after another moment of preoccupation. He stepped away from the car as his brother got in and rolled the window down.

"Hang in there, man. There's still hope."

Dillon nodded and forced a tight smile. "Thanks. I'll talk to you later."

Frank backed out of the driveway and Dillon retraced his steps to his own car. But he didn't start the engine right away. Instead he sat there, staring straight ahead.

What the hell was he going to do? How could he choose between Jessy and Zoey?

"Toss a coin?" he said facetiously.

There was no question that Zoey would be sacrificed if he stepped aside and let her go ahead with her plans not to give Miflin the pictures. The consequences of not complying with that subpoena were clear-cut.

But wasn't that what he should do? Shouldn't Jessy come before Zoey? Wouldn't a good father put his child first?

Yes. Of course. Certainly, he couldn't do it the other way around and sacrifice Jessy for Zoey. Jessy was his flesh and blood. And if he made that kind of choice and lost her, he knew he'd end up resenting Zoey. Which left only the other option—encourage Zoey not to hand over the pictures.

It was logical. It seemed the only choice. And yet his instincts told him that wasn't the answer, either.

"It's a no-win situation," he grumbled to himself as he started his car and pulled away from the curb. "And dammit, I shouldn't be in it. I *am* a good father."

How many kids were left in genuinely bad environments even when there was evidence of how bad those environments were? How could his daughter be taken away from him when he was a decent father? It just didn't make sense.

"I'm not guilty," he proclaimed to a stoplight.

So why should he act as if he were? he asked himself suddenly. It was a good question.

Why should he be worried about how those snapshots portrayed him? Most of them had been good. That should count for something. And it wasn't as if the negative ones showed him maliciously abusing her. They were just bird's-eye views of the situations that had taught him what needed to be done to make life with Jessy safer. And he had already taken steps to do just that. How could that not matter? How could it not be important?

It was important and it did matter, he decided. And he didn't believe he was just being naive. Let them lay all their worst cards out on the table. He could refute or explain them all. And if his word wasn't good enough, the court could inspect his house. They could send a social worker out once a week to check on him. He would agree to take Jessy to a doctor of the court's choice any time it was asked of him to prove that she was healthy and unhurt. Hell, he'd agree to be put under any kind of scrutiny anybody wanted, if it meant he'd get his daughter back, because he didn't have anything to hide. Not a single thing.

And if he didn't have anything to hide, why should Zoey not submit those pictures?

The opposite suddenly seemed more the case. If Zoey suppressed those snapshots, then it *would* look as if he had something to hide. And in the end he couldn't believe that was to anyone's benefit.

With his decision made, something else struck him suddenly. Not being willing to sacrifice Zoey was pretty telling. Jessy was the most important person in his life, but he realized now that she wasn't the single most important, that Zoey was on an equal level with his daughter. The only other person who had shared that had been Linda.

"It can happen twice in a lifetime," he told himself with

some surprise. Since losing Linda a part of him had believed the depth of the love he'd felt for her was a once-in-a-lifetime thing. But it wasn't true. He loved Zoey every bit as much as he had Linda. Every bit as much as he loved Jessy.

And he wanted them both in his life. Permanently.

Zoey's heart was pounding when she opened the office door to Miflin's Investigative Services. The tension she felt made it easy for her to keep a somber expression on her face. She only hoped it made her look as if she was doing something against her will, instead of being scared stiff.

She stepped into the dingy office and closed the door behind her. Several moments passed before Miflin glanced up from his desk. Recognition dawned and he raised his eyebrows at her. "Ms. Carmichael," he drawled as if he wasn't in the least surprised to see her.

"I brought the pictures," she informed him flatly.

He nodded his head, slowly, as if to say *of course you did*.

Zoey crossed to his desk, set the bulging file folder in front of him and turned to leave.

"Hold on," he said quickly. "I'll need to take a look at them."

Her heart was still pounding, but now it was in her throat.

"Have a seat, why don't you?" Miflin offered.

Oh, but he was feeling smug, Zoey thought. It was in every line of his face. She remained standing.

The investigator opened a desk drawer and took out a pair of reading glasses, the kind any pharmacy sold without a prescription. He opened the file and started to go through the photographs and negatives.

He seemed to take his time studying them one by one. Was he really moving in slow-motion to irritate her, or was she just imagining it? Zoey took a couple of deep breaths but they didn't help. Knowing what was coming, she counted the photographs as he put them on the desktop in a row. Four. Five. Six.

He stalled and she froze. With the seventh snapshot still in one hand he used the other to adjust his glasses, and craned his head forward, looking over those he had already seen and set down. Back he went to study the few that came next in the stack, then he picked up the whole bunch and shuffled through them.

His smug expression turned darker, harder. He looked up at her. "I'll bet you thought you were pretty smart. Or did you just figure I was stupid?"

She swallowed and tried to look innocent. "Excuse me?"

"You must have had some shots that made him look like Jack the Ripper."

"I don't know what you're talking about." It was a feeble lie and she knew it. But she had to play this out.

"Right." The sarcasm in his tone was as thick as mud. "These are some pretty flattering pictures. If I was as ignorant as you seem to think, I'd say our man was in line for father-of-the-year. Too bad I know enough to check the numbers on the negatives. We're missing a few."

"Not all pictures come out. I didn't see the point in bringing blackouts or blurs."

"Bull," he roared. "And you're still in contempt of court until you show me every one—whether they're blackouts or blurs or not."

All the way over here she had tried to prepare herself for his realizing what she'd done, and having to accept the consequences. Somehow it didn't keep perspiration from filming her palms, now that she was faced with it. "Those are all the pictures there are," she told him flatly.

"What did you do? Hide them? Throw them away? Burn them? Put them in a safety-deposit box?"

She pointed her chin at his desktop. "That's all there is. You're welcome to search my house or call every bank in the state to ask if I have a safety-deposit box, if that makes you feel better. But what you have in front of you is the whole bunch."

He stared at her for a long while. Zoey met and matched it; if she was going to bluff she might as well do it right. Finally Miflin sat back in his chair and said, "So you'd like for me to think they're gone for good."

She just kept staring back at him, her thoughts spinning all the while. Could she be put in jail for the supposition that other pictures existed, even if no evidence could be found?

No evidence. Oh sure. Famous last words.

But before leaving home she had sprinkled the ashes around the alyssum in the terraced garden. What was there to find? Then again, she couldn't produce blackouts and blurs, either. If she couldn't fill in the blanks maybe that was enough proof in itself. What happened to a person who destroyed evidence? Were the consequences even worse than for just not handing it over?

She felt a drop of perspiration run down her side. Still Miflin watched her as if that would be enough to make her tell him the truth. Zoey didn't think she had ever felt as transparent as she did at that moment. With nothing else to do but see the bluff through, she stood on legs that were actually shaking. "Our business is finished, Mr. Miflin."

"I hope you don't expect to be paid for this," he snarled.

Zoey didn't answer him. Instead she turned and headed for the door. With her hand on the knob he said, "I'm always glad to send a little fresh meat to the lady's jail. They ought to like a bleeding heart like you. They'll eat you alive."

She didn't say anything. All she wanted was to get out of there. She opened the door, half expecting the investigator to rush over and block her way. *I've been watching too much television,* she thought as she stepped out into the hallway. Still, it wasn't in the least heartening to hear

Miflin's voice just as she closed the door. "Not smart, lady. Not smart, at all."

Zoey was afraid the police would be waiting on her doorstep when she got home. But instead it was Dillon who was sitting on the stoop, his long legs bent at the knee, an elbow on each, his hands dangling loosely between.

He had changed clothes. Now he wore faded jeans and a white sport shirt. He was clean-shaven and his hair was combed. He looked fresh and inviting and as she pulled into the driveway and stopped the car, all Zoey could think of was getting them both behind a locked door. Unfortunately, nervousness and not the way Dillon looked caused it.

He frowned at her as she got out and walked up to the house. "Where have you been, Carmichael?"

"Have you been waiting long?" she asked rather than answer him, hurrying to unlock the front door.

"I told you not to go out of the house. I've been sitting here wondering if I should call the police and ask about recent arrests."

She stepped inside. "I wasn't arrested." *Yet.*

He followed her and she nearly slammed the door closed behind him. He glanced over his shoulder in that direction, looking confused, but didn't mention anything. Instead he said, "So. Where were you?"

For the first time she wondered how he was going to react to what she'd done. The chance that he might not like it didn't help her tension any. Stalling, she set her purse and keys on the kitchen table and then tucked her red camp shirt into her jeans, even though it didn't need it. Without turning to look at him she said, "I brought the pictures to Miflin—"

But that was as far as she got before he cut her off. "Good," he interrupted, surprising her.

"Good?" She pivoted slowly to find a serious expression on his face. Since she hadn't explained what she had done, his only assumption could be that she had delivered all of the pictures. Why was that good?

"I'm glad you did it," he said, briefly telling her about his conversation with his brother. "I decided when I left," he went on, "that I may not be the perfect parent—at least not yet—but I don't have anything to hide, Zoey, and I won't act like I do. Not handing over those pictures could only make it seem like they show something worse than what's really in them. I called Frank and talked this over with him. After seeing it my way he agreed that the truth was the best route. We can defend what's there in front of the judge's face, but there's no defense against what he might imagine. So I came down here to drive you to the investigator's office myself." He paused and gave her a crooked smile. "After I asked you something more important."

"Oh, no," she breathed, wondering if a person's head could blow up from tension, because hers felt as if it might. "You don't understand..."

He was standing directly in front of her now and he shook his head and cut her off with a finger pressed to her lips. "I don't have to understand why you did it. I'm sure your reasons were as good as your reasons for taking the pictures in the first place. What's more important is that this morning when I thought I had to choose between you and Jessy I discovered that I couldn't. I realized how much I love you, Zoey. As much as I love Jessy. And I want you in my life just the same. I want you to marry me."

Marry? Had he just said marry? Where did that come from? But he was still talking, and Zoey tried to concentrate on what he was saying.

"I know this is a rotten time to propose, but I can't help that. I want you with me to face this fight and all the rest that ever come our way." His smile broadened and he took her shoulders in his hands, squeezing, smoothing circles with his thumbs. "I've really shocked you, haven't I? Your eyes are as big as moons. But it makes sense, Zoey. Actually it makes more sense than deciding to get married when everything is going well. If we can still fall in love and want each other in the middle of all this garbage, then what we feel has to be pretty strong. I know it is for me, and I think it is for you, too. Now that the die is cast with those pictures, we can go face-first into this damn fight together.''

"Dillon, I didn't take *all* the pictures to Miflin," she blurted out.

His smile faded. His eyebrows pulled together in a frown. "What do you mean?"

"After you left I decided that no matter what you or your brother said, this situation was a wrong against you that I couldn't contribute to." She swallowed the tension that was clogging her throat. "So I burned the bad ones and submitted only the good ones. And then I mulched the garden with the ashes."

His grip on her shoulders loosened. He closed his eyes and Zoey saw his jaw tightened. "You didn't."

"I did. I thought that that way if the pictures did anything, they'd help your side." But she said it feebly, remembering that the first thing Miflin had assumed was that the missing pictures made Dillon look as bad as Jack the Ripper. "I thought it would help," she repeated.

"And what happened?" he asked in a voice that sounded as if he was working hard to keep it level.

"Miflin checked the numbers on the negatives and figured it out."

"And filled in the blanks with the worst," he finished as if her tone, alone, had told him the details.

"Yes," she admitted reluctantly. "It didn't occur to me that that would happen, even if he did figure out there were pictures missing."

He let go of her and began to pace, jabbing his fingers through his hair. "I don't believe this," he said to himself. "It's a damn comedy of errors. Bad to worse."

"I'm sorry," she offered, hearing for herself just how empty it seemed under the circumstances.

"Why didn't you just wait like I wanted you to?"

"I didn't think it should be your decision to put me in jeopardy. And I thought you would probably be reluctant to suggest or support anything that might. It seemed like my responsibility to take." She shrugged. "So I took it."

He closed his eyes and pinched the bridge of his nose. "And now you're in contempt of court."

"And your case looks worse," she put in. It was Zoey's turn to close her eyes, as if that would make the problem go away. When she opened them Dillon was facing the front door, his right hand splayed against the wood, his head down as if he were staring at his feet. Zoey felt as if she could see the burden she had just dropped on the back of those broad shoulders. "I didn't mean to do anything to hurt your chances of getting Jessy. Call your brother and tell him what I've done. Tell him I'm willing to be a witness or whatever. I'll admit that I burned the pictures and tell them what was in them."

He breathed an unamused chuckle. "A confession. Then you'll be in trouble, for sure, and if the other side has even an inkling that we're personally involved, no one will believe you. It'll just look as if you're lying for me." He shook his head. "Dammit, I wish you had waited."

"Well, I didn't, and there's nothing either one of us can do about it now," she shouted. But it was herself she was mad at, not him. She took a breath and held it, tamping down her feelings so that when she spoke again her voice was matter-of-fact. "I'll do whatever has to be done to make this right. I'll swear under oath to what was in the burned pictures. I'll take a lie-detector test. You just do anything your brother tells you to, anything it takes to win your case and I'll deal with whatever I have to on my own."

He raised his head and pushed away from the wall all in one movement, spinning around to look at her with a frown.

"That's where this whole thing started, remember? I don't want either of us fighting anything from separate corners. I want us dealing with this and everything else together. I want you to marry me."

Zoey's palms were as damp now as they had been in Miflin's office. "We can't talk about that now," she hedged. She also couldn't look him in the eye, so she glanced away from him, staring at the tramp as she went on. "And this isn't something we can fight together. Even if I didn't know it before, we were on opposite sides. The only thing our facing it together will accomplish is just what you said—it'll show that we're involved and that I'm probably lying for you. I think what we need to do now is keep as much distance between us as possible. It's important that my burning the pictures comes out as just what it was—a decision I made on my own because I believed they gave the wrong impression of you as a father. It has to be clear that you weren't involved in it. That it wasn't a cover-up."

"I don't want you to go up against this by yourself," he said again, more forcefully.

"Do you want to lose Jessy?" she demanded curtly, looking at him.

"You know the answer to that."

"Then you don't have a choice. I'll be all right. I can take care of myself."

"I don't doubt that. But just because you can, doesn't mean you should have to."

"It does in this. There's no other way."

His eyes met and locked with hers for a long moment. Then he shook his head, and yet it was clear he was accepting that she was right. He crossed to her and took her by the shoulders again.

"I hate this," he said through a clenched jaw.

"It's the only way," she reiterated.

After another moment he sighed. "I know, dammit, I know."

Zoey's hand went to his chest, answering the need to touch him and yet unable to do more than that, as if distance had already been put between them. Why did things have to be so complicated? And then he made them even more so.

"If we can't do anything else, though, we can at least talk about marriage—off the record."

Zoey couldn't help looking up into his face and the minute she did she felt as if fingers closed around her heart. Why did he have to be so handsome? Why did he have to look at her with those piercing blue eyes that told her how much he wanted her? Why did he have to be such a disarming mixture of strength and sensitivity? Why did she have to love him so much? And why did he have to bring up marriage?

"Even off the record, this is no time to consider that," she said. "Everything is in flux. Jessy has to be the most important thing on both of our minds. It's no time to think about anything else."

He frowned at her once more, but this time it was mild. "That's not how I feel," he told her softly, his voice a deep, intimate rasp. "Jessy is only half of what's most important. But if you'd rather know everything is settled and my head is clear before we talk about it, I can understand that. Let it wait."

Thick warmth radiated from his hands into her shoulders and all the way through her body, but she fought the urge to relax in his arms. "In the meantime," she forced words out of her throat, "we shouldn't have any contact. There's no way to tell if Miflin is watching or, like you said this morning, if the phones are tapped. I don't think he suspects that we have anything to do with one another yet. He thinks I refused to give him the pictures because I have some long-distance crush on the way you looked through my viewfinder. But if he finds out we spent time together or have any connection, he's bound to bring it out in the open."

Dillon nodded, but he looked reluctant. "I wish you

weren't right about all of this, but I think you are.'' He cupped her face and brought it up for a brief kiss. Then he wrapped his arms around her and pulled her close, resting his head on top of hers. If he felt the stiffness in her, he didn't show it. ''No matter what, though, if you need me I want you to call.''

She wouldn't, but rather than lie she didn't answer at all. Instead she pushed herself out of the tender trap of his arms and said firmly, ''If it comes down to it, I want you to think of Jessy first.''

''I'm going to do everything I can to make sure it doesn't come down to that.''

He reached for her again and as much as she told herself she should elude him, she couldn't do it. Instead she let him pull her back into his arms, at the same time saying, ''You better go, Dillon. I've botched things up enough. I don't want to take any more chances.''

''It's going to be a long five days until that hearing,'' he said by way of an answer, holding her so tightly she felt as though he would pull her inside of his skin if he could.

Zoey couldn't resist curling her arms up under his and filling her hands with his wide, hard back. ''I'm sorry for all of this,'' she said in barely a whisper.

''So am I.''

He leaned back and tipped her face up, lowering his mouth to hers in a deep, intimate kiss. Then he groaned and ended it. ''If I don't get out of here I'm never going to be able to.''

They let go of one another at the same time and Dillon headed for the door. But before he went through it he stopped and glanced back at her. ''I love you, Zoey.''

She swallowed. ''I love you, too,'' she admitted, knowing all the while that it was only going to make things harder.

Chapter Eleven

When would she ever learn? Zoey asked herself as she got into her car in Mayco's parking lot Thursday afternoon. In all of the upheaval Wednesday morning she had completely forgotten her ten o'clock interview for the women's clothes and shoes account. In fact, it had been late yesterday afternoon before she'd remembered it. Profuse apologies to the secretary in the advertising department after everyone else had left for the day had garnered her the appointment from which Zoey had just left. But it had been too late. Another photographer had been hired. And because of her preoccupation at Monday's interview and this, it was obvious Mayco's ad people had their doubts about her professionalism.

The blunder to beat all blunders was how she'd thought during the past four days, and again she wondered when she would learn. "What does it take to sink into your thick skull, Carmichael?" she asked her reflection in the rearview mirror as she backed out of the parking space and headed home.

She'd charged in to take care of things all on her own again, not considering anything else. And where had it ended? In contempt of court, messing up Dillon's case and forgetting an interview that was the most important thing to happen to her career since she'd come back from Africa. A short involvement with one man and his daughter and she was right back into the same trap she had been determined to avoid after Carl's death.

"Bills don't get paid and careers don't get made by putting other things first," she said aloud as she went through the last traffic light before home. And she was determined to rebuild her business. No matter what.

But there was more to it than just practicality. As much as she had loved Carl and as abhorrent as the idea of divorcing him had been, she couldn't deny that separating from him had occurred to her at her darkest moments. She'd felt so lost, so empty, so out of touch with herself, so aimless and unfulfilled that it had been a chore to get up every morning and face another day of nothing but meeting someone else's needs. It wasn't something she wanted to repeat.

"Maybe that's why all this happened," she told herself quietly. Maybe the situation with Dillon had been so disastrous because it was some sort of omen or sign. Certainly it was a blinding reminder of what she meant to avoid. And maybe it had come now before she got in any deeper with Dillon. Before it was too late.

Her house came into view, and as had happened repeatedly since her meeting with Miflin the morning before, she was relieved to see no sign of a police car out front.

But even so a part of her—a very small part—wished whatever was going to happen would, just to get it over with. She hadn't spoken to a soul other than Mayco's people since Dillon had left the day before, and she didn't have any idea what was going on. Or what to expect. As a result, she hadn't answered her doorbell once without peeking through the front window first. And between worrying about imminent arrest and the Mayco account she hadn't slept more than two hours the whole night.

She stopped the car in the driveway and got out, dragging her portfolio from the passenger seat. It was hot for so late in September, and Zoey was tired. But as tempting as a nap sounded she rejected the idea as she opened the screen and put her key in the lock on the front door. If she slept now she wouldn't be able to tonight, and darkness made all her problems seem more ominous.

"Ms. Carmichael."

Zoey jumped and jerked around at the sound of the voice from behind her. Harold Miflin. "Where did you come from?"

"Around the side of the house," he said with a smirk and a tip of his head in that direction. "I rang your bell and when there was no answer I figured sooner or later you either had to go out or come home, so I moved my car and waited for you."

Zoey was too tired and frazzled for politeness. "What do you want?"

"I came to extend an invitation."

"An invitation," she repeated suspiciously. Was this his attempt at a clever way to take her off to jail? Did he have that kind of authority?

"The Whites want to meet you."

Miflin's words echoed in her mind for only a moment before the wheels started spinning. What if they had seen her in Dillon's car the day he'd taken Jessy back? One glimpse of her now would alert them to her connection with their son-in-law and give them even more ammunition. Then she remembered that Dillon's car windows were heavily tinted. She didn't think they would have been able to see her. But still the prospect didn't sit well. "Why do they want to meet me?" she asked.

"They didn't say."

"I can't think of anything the Whites and I would have to talk about," she hedged.

The investigator shrugged negligently, as if it didn't matter to him one way or another whether she answered the request. "Maybe you can save yourself more complications."

Or maybe they just wanted to threaten her in person.

Then something else occurred to her. Maybe she could persuade them that the pictures she'd turned over to Miflin really were all that existed, and get them to accept it.

The detective must have seen her waver. "I can drive you."

"No thanks," she said without having to think about it. At this point the idea of spending any time with the man was repugnant.

"Suit yourself." He handed her a slip of paper. "That's the address, in case you decide to go." Then he gave her another of his smug smiles and left.

Zoey glanced down at the slip of paper in her hand, debating what to do. Could this mess be made any worse?

It could if Dillon's in-laws somehow realized she was involved with him. But barring that, which she didn't think was a viable possibility anyway, she hung onto the hope that the situation could be made better.

Besides, any kind of action was preferable to sitting on her thumbs, waiting for something to happen.

The Whites' house seemed bigger to Zoey as she went up the front steps and rang the bell. The maid who answered wore a blank expression, and for a moment after she had told the uniformed woman who she was, Zoey wasn't sure she was going to let her in.

"I'm the photographer," she felt obliged to add.

"Come in, please." The maid finally stepped out of the way, closing the door behind Zoey and then heading to a double door on the left. "Mr. and Mrs. White are waiting for you in here."

Tension filled Zoey as she followed the woman.

"Zowy!" Jessy spotted her before she realized the little girl was in the living room with the two attractive, sophisticated-looking older people.

"Jessy," Zoey greeted back unenthusiastically. Somehow she had assumed she wouldn't see the little girl. How was she going to explain the child knowing her?

"You come over my house to play?" Jessy said, rushing up to her.

"Sorry, honey. I came to see your grandma and grandpa."

"Mop and Popop," Jessy renamed them as if correcting Zoey.

"Miss Carmichael." The man who had stood when she entered the room came to her then, his hand extended. "I'm Richard White and this is my wife, Evelyn."

"Hello," was all Zoey answered. She could hardly say it was a pleasure to meet them.

Richard White looked past her. "Take Jessica up to her room now, please," he told the maid.

"Zowy, you wanna comin' see my horse, Tom?"

Zoey couldn't resist reaching a hand to the little girl's curly head where a mauve ribbon matched the ruffly, starched dress she wore and made her look unlike the rambunctious two-and-a-half-year-old she was. "Maybe another time, Jess."

"Aw, come on," she coaxed as if Zoey were the child.

Mrs. White stepped in, placing a firm hand on the little shoulder and urging Jessy in the direction of the maid. "The grown-ups need to talk now, Jessica. You can go and have one of those cupcakes we bought this morning."

The child accepted that. "Bye, Zowy," she said and charged ahead of the maid.

"Please come and sit down," Mr. White invited.

Zoey followed Mrs. White's lead, sitting in a wing chair that matched the one her hostess took. Mr. White propped a thigh on the arm of the sofa that faced them.

"How does Jessica know you?" Mrs. White asked.

Zoey swallowed and tried to think of a reason. Mr. White saved the day.

"Remember Miss Carmichael's name was on the police report as having found and returned her?"

"Oh, of course."

Zoey breathed again. "You have a lovely home," she said then, when what she wanted was to ask why she was here. She was glad when Richard White launched into it after his wife thanked her for the compliment.

"Mr. Miflin believes that you omitted some of the pictures."

"Yes, I know he does," Zoey answered noncommittally.

"I hope that isn't true."

Mrs. White spoke then. "Harold Miflin believes that you had doubts about whether Jessica should continue to be kept from her father, and we thought it might help for you to see what she has here with us."

"We wanted you to know that we've done this not to hurt Jessica's father, but to further her best interest," the older man put in.

"I'm sure," Zoey said, realizing as she did that she believed it. On the end table beside the couch was a framed picture of a woman whose resemblance to both Jessy and Mrs. White was enough to tell Zoey she was Linda. Young, attractive, happy, vital. Her death was a tragedy. And out of that had come another tragedy for everyone involved.

Mrs. White was speaking again. "If Harold is right and you have pictures of Jessica in situations that aren't ideal, please don't withhold them. This isn't a criminal case against her father, so you don't have to worry about that. We just want what's best for our granddaughter and we think this home—her mother was raised here, and her grandfather and I are here for her all the time—is a much better environment than a home with a single father who travels out of state on business. It isn't that we think Dillon

is a bad person, and I'm sure your pictures don't show that.
It's just a matter of the better of two households.''

"I understand that, Mrs. White," Zoey said. She also
agreed, it was a matter of the better of two households.
And from Jessy's standpoint, Zoey believed Dillon's won.

As houses went, Dillon's might not look like a two-and-
a-half-year-old lived there yet, but it looked like one she
could live in. This place was beautiful, but it had a museum
quality about it. Zoey couldn't picture Jessy living here at
all. Visiting—on her best behavior—maybe. But not happily living here with her natural exuberance allowed to run
free.

And as for the people themselves? The Whites seemed
calm, kind and loving, but very formal. They were no
match for a father who blew raspberries on her bare stomach or got down on all fours to play with her or carted her
around on his shoulders.

"I know what Mr. Miflin thinks," Zoey went on. "But
in spite of that, there just aren't any other pictures for me
to give you." The older couple stared at her but didn't say
anything for so long Zoey felt compelled to add, "I'm
sorry."

"You do realize that it isn't your place to make a judgment, don't you, Miss Carmichael?" the older man said,
his tone of voice more businesslike.

"I realize that I can't produce pictures I don't have."

"We'd be willing to pay you whatever you wanted,"
Mrs. White put in, sounding just a little desperate.

"I'm afraid no amount of money can change the way
things are. I'm sorry," she repeated. "I know how important this is to you both."

"Maybe you should think it over," Mr. White said in a
vaguely intimidating way.

Was he threatening her? Zoey wondered. It didn't matter.
She'd been living with that all week. "I don't have to think
it over." She stood. "I've given Mr. Miflin everything I
have. That's all I can do."

Zoey took a step toward the door and then stopped. "You're wrong, you know," she said, looking directly at them both. "If you honestly want what's best for Jessy you'll let her father raise her. What my pictures show is a man who loves his daughter every bit as much as you say you do. He takes time with her, he's patient, he teaches her, plays with her, protects her, he...Well, it looks to me as if Jessy is lucky to have a father like that. Personally I think it would be a shame to rob her of him."

The silence that fell then seemed heavier than any before. Mrs. White stared at her. Mr. White arched an eyebrow in a way that gave Zoey the impression he was outraged at her audacity.

"I don't think we have anything more to say to one another, Miss Carmichael," he said.

Zoey just nodded and left. It wasn't until she had started her car and pulled away from the house that she wondered why Dillon's in-laws were pressing so hard for those missing pictures when they had the ammunition of reports from a doctor and a psychologist.

The bedroom set that Jessy had picked out Monday night was delivered early Thursday afternoon. To Dillon it was a godsend, because assembling it gave him something to do beside pace and worry and watch Zoey's house for a sign of her.

He took his toolbox out of the closet at the foot of the stairs and went up to Jessy's room to dismantle the crib. Baby smell greeted him—the mingling scents of powder, lotion, new diapers and the plastic that made up most of her toys and dolls. For a moment he stood in the doorway and just breathed it in. It was hard to believe this would one day turn into the smell of perfume and hair spray, but he had enough experience with his nieces to know it was inevitable. And it jabbed at him to realize how much of Jessy's babyhood he had missed.

After setting down his toolbox he stripped the bedding

and lifted out the still-new mattress. Then he took the pliers and screwdriver and turned his attention to the frame.

The top rail at one end was marred with tiny indentations where Jessy had cut her two front teeth. Dillon ran his thumb across the mark, smiling at the mental image of those little white nibs, which had appeared when she was five months old.

There wasn't another nick or scratch on the crib. How could there be when Jessy had used it during those first six months of her life and then not again until last week? And for a second time he felt cheated.

"Guess I'll have to make up for it with the kids Zoey and I will have," he told Arachnid, who was watching from the doorway with his head on the floor between his paws.

As always, the thought of a fresh start helped. Marriage to Zoey, and a couple more kids along with Jessy, all filling this big, empty house with warm bodies and happy voices again. How would Jessy react to sharing the attention with a new baby? Not as badly if she lived here instead of with the Whites.

He collapsed the crib, aware that the knot was in his stomach again; that it was tough to keep his mind on those fresh starts, with the custody mess still hanging over his head. What was going on with Zoey? he wondered as he moved the crib out the door. Had she been called to testify? Was she being hounded for those missing pictures?

In the basement he wrapped two tarps around the baby bed to protect it, assuring himself that it wouldn't be down there long before he and Zoey would need it. But then he wondered if he really could go on to have other kids if he lost Jessy. And how the hell was he going to be able to wait until next week this way?

The phone was ringing when he went back upstairs. The sound of his brother's voice on the other end answered his hello.

"Don't tell me. The hearing has been postponed again," Dillon guessed.

"Geez, don't I even get a 'hi, how are you?'"

"Hi. How are you?" Dillon repeated flatly.

"Real good, thanks. Sharon and I decided to go to Hawaii in February to get out of the cold and snow. Facing winter seems a lot easier since I just picked up brochures full of pictures of palm trees and sandy beaches."

"It's ninety degrees today, Frank. How can you be sweating and dreading winter at the same time?"

"Who's sweating? My office is air-conditioned."

It was irrational, but Dillon found his brother's enthusiastic tone irritating. "Did you call for a reason or just to brag about your vacation plans?"

"Testy, testy. What are you doing, mowing the grass?"

"No, I'm not mowing the grass. I just took Jessy's crib down and now I have to put up her new bed and dresser."

"So, you got her one. I'll tell Sharon her services aren't needed. What did you get?"

Dillon rolled his eyes to the ceiling. He knew his brother wouldn't call just to chat and yet when Frank was playing this kind of game there was no way around it. "She picked out a *Sesame Street* motif. We have Bert and Ernie and Big Bird and Cookie Monster all over the place."

"Bad move. She'll outgrow that stuff in a couple of years and you'll have to go out and buy new furniture all over again. You should have waited for Sharon to go with you."

"It was what Jessy wanted," Dillon groused and then stopped, hoping silence would prompt his brother to get to the point.

"So, have you heard from Fun City yet on your designs for their new park?"

Dillon sighed loudly. "They're buying them all, and asking for three more."

"Wow. Great. How come you didn't call and tell me the good news? I'd think you'd be jumping up and down over this."

"I've had other things on my mind," Dillon understated.

"No? You have?"

"This is really funny, Frank. I can hardly stand up I'm laughing so hard. But I have work to do and I know you didn't call just to be cute. So why don't you tell me the reason we're having this afternoon gabfest?"

"You know, a guy not as good-natured as me might take offense at your tone. In fact someone with a malicious streak might just hang up and leave you wondering about what he called to tell you in the first place."

"Say it, Frank," Dillon nearly shouted in frustration.

"Keep your pants on." Frank let silence lapse, but when it became obvious that Dillon wasn't going to fill it, he said, "So," and then let another extended pause play the part of a drumroll. "How would you like to pick Jessy up in an hour, lock, stock and teddy bears, and move her back home for good?"

Zoey had just put her portfolio away when there was a knock on her back door. Actually it was more like a beating on her back door. As she rushed to it she had visions of someone being chased and needing refuge in a hurry. But when she opened it what she found was Dillon, working to keep a grin from stretching all the way to his earlobes.

"You're not suppose to be here," she reminded him.

He looked around as if making sure he hadn't been followed and said in a stage whisper, "It's all right. We're safe." Then he opened the screen and came in.

"Have you had a close encounter with laughing gas?" she asked.

"Just a phone call."

"You've won the lottery," she guessed.

"Better."

"Nothing is better."

"Getting my daughter back is."

That knocked the air out of her. But in a good way. "What?"

He laughed. "Frank just called and told me I can pick

her up in an hour—lock, stock and teddy bears, was how
he put it.''

"Well, don't just stand there. Give me the details."

"It seems that my in-laws didn't have a leg to stand on.
They made their accusations without any real reason, except just what I thought—they couldn't stand to lose Jessy.
Then they hired your Harold Miflin to get them any kind
of evidence he could to make me look bad—that wasn't
the way they put it, but that's the gist of it. Apparently he
hadn't had any luck so in a last-ditch effort he hired you,
hoping constant surveillance through picture-taking might
turn up something.'' Dillon winked at her. "And you, Carmichael, singlehandedly saved me from going through the
hearing and possibly losing Jessy."

"I did?"

"On two counts. One, by not turning in the shots that
made me look bad, you left them without any evidence."

"But what about the reports from the doctor and psychologist?"

Dillon's grin grew broader. "Miflin lied."

"Your in-laws hadn't paid for them?"

"Nope. In fact, my demanding to know about them was
the first Richard had heard of them. Apparently Miflin
made it all up to convince you I was a rotten father, so
you'd deliver the pictures."

Miflin lied. Zoey mentally chewed on that for a moment,
wondering why it hadn't occurred to her before. The investigator had lied about Jessy being taken away from Dillon, and he had lied by omission about who he worked for.
Why wouldn't he have lied about those reports, too? "Of
course." Then she remembered he'd said there were two
counts on which she'd helped. "What else did I do?"

He grinned. "Apparently you gave a rousing speech in
my favor that convinced them I'm a pretty terrific father."

"Yes, I did," she confirmed, still a little dumbfounded
by all of this. She moved to the kitchen table and sat down

on the edge of one of the chairs. "Then you get Jessy back and I'm off the hook?"

"Better than off the hook. You saved the day."

Zoey shook her head. It was all too good to be true. Then she remembered his referring to the Whites as if they'd spoken. "How did you find this out?"

"When I got off the phone with Frank I made a call to my father-in-law. I thought I had the right to know just what's been going on. Of course he made it sound as if it had all been done out of deep concern for Jess. He referred to the whole thing as his and Evelyn's need for reassurance that I could raise my daughter without Linda—like some test that he was glad I'd passed with flying colors, thanks to whatever it was you said to them. And Miflin took the blame for a lot, although, as I said, Richard did seem genuinely confused about the medical-reports business."

"I think Miflin deserved a lot of the blame." For a moment Zoey just let it all sink in. "So, that's it. It's all over with?"

"All but some paperwork."

"And I'm not in danger of becoming a convict?"

"A wife, yes, but definitely not a convict."

Zoey couldn't help going very still, and the sudden silence in the room seemed strange after Dillon's enthusiasm.

He pulled a chair out and sat in it, facing her. Very gently, he took both of her hands between his own. "What do you say, Zoey? Make this day complete for me. Tell me you'll marry me and the three of us will be a family."

It was unnerving to realize just how tempting that idea was. His hands were big and warm around hers, and he smelled of after-shave. A part of her just wanted to melt into his arms, to say yes and walk up that hill and be a part of his and Jessy's lives. It would be so easy.

But then falling into traps always was. And fresh in her mind were these past few days and her close brush with what had made her miserable before.

"I can't," she said very, very softly, unable to look at him.

The silence that came then was heavier, harder to bear.

After a moment Dillon said, "What do you mean you can't?"

"I told you I need to be selfish, to concentrate on my work."

"Fine. I'm all for it."

"I can't do that and be married, too."

"Why not?" The joy that had been in his voice before had evolved into disbelief.

Zoey pulled her hands out of his and stood, hanging on tight to her elbows as if it was the only way not to reach out to him. "Marriage is a trap for me, Dillon. I get in way over my head in putting someone else first, in meeting other people's needs and ignoring my own, in just being responsible for everything. So far over that I feel like I'm drowning or suffocating." She raised her hands as if to ward him off. "This whole past week is an example...or maybe a reminder to me. But look at it—I was willing to go to jail for you. I was so caught up in the whole thing, that I forgot that interview I had scheduled for Wednesday morning and lost a big job because of it."

"I'm sorry. I forgot about the interview, too."

"You don't have to apologize. It isn't your fault. It's the situation, you see. And the fact that I care so much about you and Jessy, too. But this situation was temporary. It's over now. Marriage is permanent and I can't do it again. It makes me unhappy and..." Her voice tapered off with an admission she had never made before, not even to herself. "I'd end up resenting you, the way I resented Carl."

"Did I ever say I wanted you to put me first? Or Jessy? Or our needs? That I expected you to have all the responsibility?"

"It doesn't have anything to do with you or what you want or expect."

"It has a lot to do with me. I love you."

"I love you, too," she admitted cautiously. "That's all part of the problem. If I didn't care so much it would be easier to keep my distance and my perspective. But I do care. And for me marriage is a trap I can't fall into again. That's all there is to it."

He stood and came to face her once more so that she had to look at him. It wrenched her heart to see his face creased with confusion, with disappointment, with disbelief. "I won't let you do it," he offered, taking her by the shoulders.

"You can't stop it. You tried Wednesday morning, remember? It didn't matter. I burned the pictures and went to Miflin's office with what was left, even after you had expressly told me to wait until you found out what was the best course. I could have used that time to go to my interview instead. It didn't even occur to me. The only hope I have is to avoid the pitfalls. It's like an alcoholic needing not to go into a bar. And marriage, for me, is the biggest pitfall of them all." She eased herself out of his grip. Having admitted for the first time that one of the feelings she'd had at the end of her marriage was resentment for Carl cemented her resolve not to do it again. She didn't want to end up resenting Dillon and probably Jessy, too.

She turned her back on him, still hanging on tight to her elbows, keeping her shoulders straight. "The only way I can avoid it is if I'm alone. I can't marry you, Dillon. I just can't."

"Think it over."

She shook her head. "There's nothing to think about."

For another long moment neither of them said anything, and Zoey wondered how she was going to have the strength to keep refusing him if he didn't leave soon.

Then he said, "I don't suppose it will make any difference, but just for the record, you're making a mistake. Yes, maybe this is a weakness you have, but I think that between the two of us knowing your tendency and being on the lookout for it, we could even things out. I don't believe that to marry me means you and everything you want automatically get sacrificed.''

But Zoey knew better. She'd lived it. Again she only shook her head.

"Dammit, Zoey, I love you," he shouted.

She didn't say anything to that because she couldn't speak through the lump in her throat.

"And you want me to just accept no for an answer, is that it?"

"Yes," she managed to whisper.

"I can't believe you won't even give us a chance."

"I'm sorry," she said resolutely, holding on tight to her resolve and letting it sound in her voice.

"So that's it?"

"That's it."

"You want me to walk out of here and pretend I don't know you if we happen to both come out of our houses at the same time?"

She nodded.

"Zoey..."

"Just go. Please."

Palpably tense silence once more. Then, in a loud burst of anger, Dillon said, "Fine. If that's what you want. Have it your way. I sure as hell don't want to be a trap."

She heard him leave, slamming the door behind himself.

And on top of everything else, she felt guilty for having cast a pall over a day that should have been completely joyous for him.

Chapter Twelve

The week that followed was about as miserable as they could come for Zoey. A delivery of Mayco's housewares gave her enough work to keep her busy, but somehow it didn't keep her mind off Dillon. Or her eyes from straying out the back windows and up the hill to his house a gazillion times a day. And two gazillion times a night.

She watched him mow his lawn. She watched him put up a swing set for Jessy. She watched him push his daughter on the swings, teach her to slide down the slide. She watched him build castles in the sandbox. Through that wall of windows she watched them eat more meals than she could get past the constant lump in her own throat. She even watched them attempt to bake a cake. She saw Dillon put Jessy down for every afternoon nap and get her ready for bed each night. In fact, on the first two nights Jessy was back, Zoey watched Dillon sleep with the little girl, apparently easing the way for her to get used to the new bed that had replaced her crib. Zoey knew what time Dillon went to bed himself and what time he got up in the mornings. She even knew that at least once during the middle of each night he went in to check on his daughter, because Zoey was watching then, too, not managing much sleep herself.

Maybe her own house wasn't as perfect as she had initially thought, she told herself on Tuesday morning as she sat at the kitchen table looking at proofs of coffee makers, carafes and canisters. She'd been looking at the same proof sheet for over an hour, something that ordinarily took her a few minutes, tops. But Dillon and Jessy had come all the way down to the terraced garden today, he to pick weeds from among the late-blooming flowers and she to make mud pies from a small puddle he'd dampened for her.

And Zoey wanted to be out there with them so much it hurt.

"Dammit," she muttered to herself.

Then she snatched up her purse and stormed out to her car.

"Hi, stranger," Jane greeted her fifteen minutes later when Zoey appeared at her door. "You've made yourself scarce the last week. Have you been sick?"

Did heartsick count? "No, I'm fine," she lied as she went into her sister's house.

"Come into the kitchen. I'm making a pie."

Zoey followed listlessly. "Where's Tim?"

"He's at a neighbor's birthday party, thank goodness. I yelled at him all morning, I think he needed a breather from me. I know I needed one from him." Jane leaned in for a closer look at her face. "So, what's wrong?"

"Who said anything was wrong?"

Her sister went to the table where a lump of pie crust waited on a floured board. "Your chin is dragging on the floor. Something is wrong."

Zoey watched Jane rub flour on a rolling pin. "Dillon wanted me to marry him," she blurted out.

Midway to the crust, Jane stopped and looked Zoey in the eye. "The child abuser?"

"He isn't a child abuser. In fact he got custody of his daughter without even having to go to court. The whole thing was trumped up." Zoey brought her sister up to date, complete with her reasons for turning down Dillon's proposal. "Marriage is a trap I can't fall into again," she finished. Then, frustrated with watching Jane start and stop in her attempts to roll the pie crust and listen to her story, Zoey nudged in front of her sister and took the rolling pin. "Here, let me do that before it dries out."

Jane stepped aside and started to chuckle.

"What's so funny?"

"You are. If I let you roll that crust, does that mean visiting me will qualify as a trap, too, and you won't come back?"

"Huh?"

"The whole world is a trap for you, Zoey. Why did you agree to take Carol's wedding pictures, when you didn't have the time? Because you felt responsible. Why did you spend the whole reception taking care of the buffet and the guests? Because you felt responsible. Then there was your feeling responsible for proving your neighbor was a bad guy and saving the little girl, or proving he was innocent and reuniting them—when all you were supposed to do was take some pictures. You'll never change, Zoey. You've been feeling responsible for everything and everybody as long as I've known you." Jane laughed. "You can't even come in here without feeling you have to roll my pie crust. It doesn't have anything to do with the situation or other people. It's just you."

"Fine. Roll your own pie crust," Zoey answered irascibly.

Jane replaced her and went on. "Maybe marriage seemed like the culprit because you were in Africa, with no one but Carl to do it for. But believe me, if you had been here during your marriage, you would have been doing it for all the rest of us, too, the same way you've been doing it since you got back. If you love this guy you might as well marry him, because you'll probably find a way to be responsible for him one way or another. You might as well have him in the bargain.''

It sounded so fatalistic. Probably because Zoey had never thought of it as an ingrained response and Jane was right—that was just what it was. On the other hand, she thought, if it wasn't the situation or the people, and she was the cause, she could change it, couldn't she?

"I have to go," Zoey said all of a sudden, wanting time to think about this.

"You just got here."

In spite of her sister's complaint, Zoey stood and headed for the front door. "I'll call you."

In as much of a hurry as when she had arrived, Zoey pulled out of Jane's driveway. But she didn't head directly home. Instead she took the long, scenic route, the wheels in her mind moving faster than those on her car.

Feeling responsible was definitely a common thread in her life, she realized. She'd always felt it strongly—responsible for helping her mother, for taking care of her younger brothers and sisters, for pitching in, for Carl. For everything. See a need, meet it—that was Zoey. It had begun as a hazard of growing up the oldest in a big family. And from there it had washed over into marriage and all the rest of her life.

Some of it was good, she admitted to herself. She wouldn't want to be a person who ignored the suggestion of child abuse rather than accept the responsibility of doing something about it. On the other hand, it wasn't her place to judge Dillon's fitness. It hadn't even been a part of the job. Any more than it was her place to insist he put up safer locks or feed Jessy better, or to tell Carol's photographer from which angle to shoot the wedding pictures and what lens to use. None of that was any more her place to do than rolling Jane's pie crust had been. Large issues or small ones, this was just plain out of control with her.

"You want to be a big pain-in-the-neck buttinski, Carmichael? Because that's where you're headed," she said aloud.

And why? It was one thing to put herself last when it was necessary. But Carol would still have had a wedding complete with food and pictures, no matter what. Dillon's house would have been secured for Jessy, and her diet would have been improved even without Zoey's butting in—Dillon had convinced her of that. Even the custody case would have been resolved just the same, because without any pictures at all the Whites wouldn't have had a case. In fact, she had almost made that situation worse.

"So why am I doing it?" she asked herself.

There wasn't a good reason. It was just something that had begun as a child and never stopped. But putting everyone else first did not have to be a way of life, for crying out loud. And married or not, Zoey realized it was something she had to change. For her own sake.

But as she pulled into her driveway she thought that realizing she had to change was one thing. Doing it was a tougher nut to crack. After all, it was something she did without even thinking about it; without even remembering there were other, more important things she needed to accomplish—like that interview with the women's department at Mayco's. Could she really marry Dillon and parent Jessy without feeling totally responsible for their every breath?

Feeling somewhat daunted, Zoey let herself into her house and tossed her keys on the table. The first place her glance went was out the back window to the terraced garden. Dillon had apparently just finished his work there, because his gardening tools were gone and he was picking up a very muddy and rebellious Jessy and carrying her toward their house.

Oh, how she wanted to be there with them, belonging to their little family, muddy, screaming kid and all.

She loved Dillon, she realized then, in a way she hadn't loved Carl, with more passion, more urgency, more heat. How could she ever stand not having him in her life?

She couldn't. That was all there was to it. Living without him was unthinkable. She would just have to trust that he really would support her efforts when they lagged because this was a tough nut that had to be cracked with the complication of marriage and a child.

Deciding what she wanted was easier than marching up the hill and announcing it. Especially after a week of witnessing Dillon carrying on very well without her. There hadn't been a single time through all the hours she had spent watching him that he had so much as cast a glance in the direction of her house. He looked, for all the world, as if it had taken only her refusal to make him forget her entirely.

So she hatched a plan and then waited for her moment.

She took a quick shower and washed her hair, poking her head out of the bathroom a dozen times during the process to look up the hill.

Wanting to be irresistible, she chose khaki shorts—just short enough—and a bright red tank top—just tight enough and cut in at the shoulders. Once she was dressed she finger combed her wet hair to make the most of the permanent waves. Then she applied Jane's eye shadow that she had yet to return, mascara and even a little eyeliner for dramatic effect. She finished off with blush before leaning out the door to look up the hill again.

Every day for the past four days, Jessy had spent some time riding her tricycle in the cement dog run. With the fence six-feet-high and the gate latched far above Jessy's reach, Zoey knew the little girl was safe outside alone. Zoey just hoped day five didn't break the routine.

She ducked back into the bathroom and ran a pick

through her hair, spritzing it lightly with spray to hold it. A dash of lip gloss and she was done. But when she had cleaned up the bathroom and gone out, there was still no sign of Jessy in the dog run.

What if the pattern was broken today? Would she have the courage to just walk up the hill and announce that she loved Dillon and wanted to marry him, after all? Or maybe she could go up to borrow something and hope one sight of her had him on his knees begging her to reconsider.

Not likely.

Come on out, Jessy.

As if in answer, the sliding-glass door opened and out came Jessy with Dillon fast behind. He was wearing a white T-shirt and a pair of jeans that were so faded there was only a trace of blue left in them. His clothes clung to his well-muscled body like a second skin and set Zoey's heart to palpitating. As he put Jessy in the dog run, her glance slipped from his broad shoulders to his narrow waist, tight derriere, then long, sinewy legs. He was barefoot. Somehow that seemed sexier than she could bear. She held her breath and waited for him to go back inside.

But unlike every other day, he didn't.

He set the sprinkler. He readjusted it twice, to make sure it hit a dry spot just right. He picked up some of Jessy's toys and put them in the sandbox. He threw a ball for Arachnid.

Zoey was tempted to forget her plan and just go ahead up the hill. In fact she took three steps toward the door. But sometime during those three steps she pictured him telling her he'd changed his mind. That the first proposal had come out of despair, when he'd thought he was going to lose the custody case, and the second had come out of elation, when he hadn't. But now that he'd had a chance to think about it, he wasn't sure it was such a hot idea. And she would have to make that long walk down the hill without her dignity.

She decided to wait a little longer. At least if she could

get him on her own territory, she could spare a little of her pride.

And then, just when she didn't think he would, Dillon went back in the house. Zoey watched him cross the kitchen and go through the doorway that she knew led to the laundry room. She ignored the skitter of apprehension that ran through her and went out the back door.

All the way up the hill she hugged the hedges that bordered both her property and his, keeping her eyes trained on the kitchen. She made it a few feet from the dog run before he came out of the laundry room. Zoey dived behind a bush.

I hope nobody is watching this, she thought as she hid, peeking out every few minutes to see if the coast was clear. Luck was with her, she decided, when his phone rang and he turned his back to the glass wall to answer it.

Zoey went the last distance to the dog run in a hurry.

"Hi, Jessy," she called from the bushes, her voice barely above a whisper.

The little girl looked all around before finally spotting her. "Zowy!"

"Shh." Zoey raised both of her palms to stall the little girl's outburst. "Do you want to come and jump on the tramp?"

"Yes I do," Jessy answered, running her words together.

"Okay, but you have to be real quiet. We'll make it a surprise for your dad."

Jessy didn't seem to care about that. She was only interested in getting off her tricycle and heading for the gate.

Zoey stole a glance into the kitchen. Dillon was still on the phone, his back to her. She dashed around to the other side of the run, threw open the latch on the gate and took Jessy's hand, then slinked back to the hedge. "Let's make it a secret, okay?"

"Okeydokey," Jessy agreed.

Zoey picked her up and quickly retraced her steps, glancing over her shoulder all the way to make sure Dillon didn't see her. He was still on the telephone when she made it to her back door and into her own house.

"Move it or lose it, Zowy," Jessy said when Zoey continued to look out the back window rather than lifting her onto the tramp.

"Move it or lose it?" Zoey repeated with a laugh as she finally obliged. "Where did you get that one?"

But the little girl didn't answer, intent only on jumping, her arms out to her sides as if she were flying, and her tongue pointing up toward her nose.

Zoey stood at the edge, keeping Jessy only peripherally in her vision as she watched for Dillon, her heart beating a mile a minute. It didn't take long before he hung up and went to the sliding door to look at the dog run. Then he was outside in a flash, Arachnid close on his heels. Zoey heard him call Jessy's name as he searched the yard. Then, for the first time in a week, she saw him turn his gaze directly on her house.

"Cross your fingers for me, Jessy."

Dillon's knock on her back door was only slightly louder than that of her heart. "It's open. Come in," she called.

For a moment she didn't think he would, and fear made her light-headed. But then he came in, his brow creased, his eyes barely touching on her before moving to Jessy, who seemed oblivious to the tension in the room.

"I should change her name to Houdini," he said without greeting either of them, without looking at Zoey, without any warmth in his voice. In fact there was a decided formality to his tone that made Zoey's hopes sink.

Should she confess and explain that she just wanted to get him down here? Or should she take this as a warning and leave him thinking Jessy had come on her own?

As Zoey worried, Dillon went to the side of the tramp and put his arms out for his daughter. "Come on, squirt. You can't come down here like this."

"Yessir," Jessy protested. "My Zowy said."

That decided it. She could hardly let a two-and-a-half-

year-old take the rap for her. "She's right," Zoey started.
But discovering her voice came out in a high-pitched little
squeak she stopped and took a breath. "Jessy didn't get
out this time. I stole her."

It was the first time Dillon looked directly at Zoey for
more than a split second. One eyebrow arched sardonically.
"Oh?"

She only nodded confirmation. It was hard to talk with
her heart in her throat. But she had to try. "I...uh...I
wanted to see you."

His eyebrow went up higher.

"I can be kind of blind sometimes," she began. "But
it's been pointed out to me that I charge in and take responsibility for just about everything..."

"Whether you need to or not," he put in.

"Right," she agreed uneasily. "That's just the point.
You see, I honestly believed that if I could avoid the situations where I did it the worst, I could avoid doing it
altogether."

"Situations like marriage. Or should I say traps like marriage?"

Zoey ignored his barb. "I realized today that it doesn't
have anything to do with the situation. Or the people involved or even whether or not there's a need. The trap is
inside of me, and I fall into it no matter what, where, when
or who I'm with."

For a long moment the only sound in the room was the
irregular thumps of Jessy jumping on the trampoline. Then
Dillon said, "And you just wanted me to know?"

That sounded very final. Maybe she should take it that
way, rather than sticking her neck out any further.

Before she could decide he said, "I think I could have
lived without the information, if it isn't leading to anything
better."

"It does lead to something." She couldn't make herself
say "better" just in case he didn't think it was. "You see,
today I realized that this is something I have to stop. Some-

thing I have to change inside myself, because my avoidance theory doesn't hold water.''

His eyes bored into hers, but his expression remained so fierce that it was hard for Zoey to meet them. And when he still didn't say anything, she glanced at Jessy instead. "I could use a little help, here," she said to no one in particular.

"I thought you could do everything on your own—probably including changing yourself.''

"No one else can change another person.''

"They can support the changes, though. And be the reminder when you slip into old patterns. But then I said that the last time I saw you and you didn't buy it.''

"I was wrong. About a lot of things.''

"You sure were.''

She agreed with only a nod.

"So, Carmichael.'' His voice was still gruff, but there was the faintest hint of self-mockery to it. "Did you lure me down here to propose to me?''

That helped. A lot. Zoey fought a smile and looked at him again only to find one tugging at the corners of his mouth. "I don't know. Do I have to get down on my knees?''

He shrugged just one shoulder. "It might be a nice touch.''

"Forget it,'' she said, her confidence restored by the evaporation of the tension between them.

"Okay. Do it standing there.''

"You want to marry me, Mills?''

"Not when you ask me like that, I don't.''

Zoey clasped her hands and pressed them to her chest theatrically. "Heart of my heart, love of my life, will you marry me and save me from myself?''

"Better.'' He reached over and pulled her into his arms. "Much better.''

"Is that a yes?''

He winked and gave her a lascivious, lopsided smile. "Oh yeah, definitely."

"But—"

"But what?" he cut her off.

"I want to keep this place as my studio because I'm still going all out to rebuild my business."

"Okay."

"And I have to warn you, I'm going to do everything I can *not* to be a compliant wife."

That made him laugh. "Good. I never wanted a compliant wife. You're free to tell me no anytime…except maybe in bed."

Now it was her turn to smile slyly. "I'm not giving up *all* responsibilities. Especially not when it means denying myself."

He kissed her, short, quick. "And just in case it's on your mind, I don't expect you to carry all the responsibility for Jessy, either. For instance, if she's sick and one of us needs to stay home with her we'll decide based on which of us can miss work more easily that day. I want every responsibility shared. Understood?"

She thought about it for a minute. "Feels kind of good knowing I don't have to carry it all."

He pulled her in tighter and the teasing tone dropped out of his voice. "Everything about this feels kind of good. I love you, Zoey."

"I love you, too, Dillon. This last week was awful. It was agony to watch you and Jessy and not be a part of your family."

He grinned. "I'm glad to hear all that yard work didn't go unnoticed."

"You mean you did it on purpose?"

"Would I do a thing like that?"

"I don't know. Would you?"

He nuzzled her neck. "Without giving it a second thought."

"So you figured just the sight of you was going to tempt me out of my mind, huh?"

He rocked his hips into hers. "I was hoping."

Zoey swallowed the instant desire that rose inside of her, and closed her eyes. "Well, you were right," she said in a huskier tone.

His breath was warm against her ear, his voice intimate. "What are we going to do about it?"

"You guys wanna jup?" Jessy asked as if on cue, making both adults laugh.

"No, thanks, sweetheart," Dillon answered his daughter.

"I don't think there's anything we can do about it until Jessy goes to sleep tonight," Zoey whispered in his ear.

"She's going to have the earliest bedtime of her life, then."

"I doan wanna go to bed, Dad."

Dillon groaned and cupped Zoey's rear to pull her discreetly up against him. "She doesn't want to go to bed," he repeated with a grimace.

"There's plenty of time, you know," she said as she nibbled his earlobe.

"Wrong. I want this fresh start on its way."

"Fresh start?"

"That's what it is, isn't it? A fresh start at a family for Jess. A fresh start at love for you and me. A fresh start at being irresponsible for you."

"I don't think I want to be irresponsible. Just enough less responsible so I can breathe and have a life of my own."

"I'm all for it. The last thing I want you to do is suffocate and resent me. I want us to have the rest of our lives together, breathing and happy."

Zoey smiled and laid her head against his heart. "Making sure of that is something I don't mind being responsible for," she told him just before his lips found hers.

"So." His voice had lost all teasing. "There aren't any traps here, Carmichael. Know that. I only want what's best for you. If that means all three kids, and I come dead last some of the time, it's okay."

"Three kids?"

"I thought it was a nice number."

"Better than eleven."

"Eleven would definitely be a trap I couldn't save either of us from." He kissed the top of her head. "I mean it. No traps. No pitfalls. Just the two of us working at everything together. Agreed?"

"Agreed."

Zoey closed her eyes and listened to his heartbeat, steady, even, strong. If loving him was a trap it was as tender as they came, and she couldn't imagine ever minding falling into it.

* * * * *

SPECIAL EDITION

Stories of love and life, these powerful
novels are tales that you can identify with—
romances with "something special" added
in!

Fall in love with the stories of authors such
as **Nora Roberts, Diana Palmer, Ginna Gray**
and many more of your special favorites—as
well as wonderful new voices!

Special Edition brings you
entertainment for the heart!

SSE-GEN

SILHOUETTE®

Desire®

Do you want...

Dangerously handsome heroes

Evocative, everlasting love stories

Sizzling and tantalizing sensuality

Incredibly sexy miniseries like **MAN OF THE MONTH**

Red-hot romance

Enticing entertainment that can't be beat!

You'll find all of this, and much *more* each and every month in **SILHOUETTE DESIRE**. Don't miss these unforgettable love stories by some of romance's hottest authors. Silhouette Desire—where your fantasies will always come true....

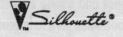

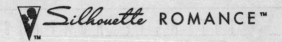

What's a single dad to do when he needs a wife by next Thursday?

Who's a confirmed bachelor to call when he finds a baby on his doorstep?

How does a plain Jane in love with her gorgeous boss get him to notice her?

From classic love stories to romantic comedies to emotional heart tuggers, **Silhouette Romance** offers six irresistible novels every month by some of your favorite authors! Such as...beloved bestsellers **Diana Palmer, Annette Broadrick, Suzanne Carey, Elizabeth August** and **Marie Ferrarella**, to name just a few—and some sure to become favorites!

Fabulous Fathers...Bundles of Joy...Miniseries... Months of blushing brides and convenient weddings... Holiday celebrations... You'll find all this and much more in **Silhouette Romance**—always emotional, always enjoyable, always about love!